REAL MUMS,
REAL STRUGGLES,
REAL LOVE,
REAL JESUS.

Dear. Heather.

That ju All the work
you did For the Lord.
I appreal this
ANEN.
KAUsTV~.

For my parents

Introduction by KoHsin Illingworth

Books are written from our heart and I want to dedicate this book to my Lord and my Saviour JESUS CHRIST. Thank you JESUS who gave me this vision in the very beginning in the year of 2016. That was when I was deeply suffering Post Natal depression with my daughter Hannah. The very beginning of the desire comes from knowing I prayed for a child and went through a difficult pregnancy then I was hit with post natal depression while some people told me I am not allowed to complain about motherhood because my child is a miracle. That hit me hard! When I pray to God for seeking the truth I have discovered motherhood is messy, but at the same time mothers are designed to love and protect their children. Being a journalist myself I am always curious to find out the truth. The truth is that the majority of earthly parents will try to do their best for their children, but not all of them. Some of them sadly abandon their children. So as a believer I believe our heavenly Father truly cares for us and Jesus wants to bless us with children. It is the Lord who gave me the desire to write this book in the first place and Jesus helped me to reach completion. I am so thankful that many prayer friends are praying over this book and so grateful for these real mums who gave me their consent to publish their testimony!

During this process of writing this book, personally I struggled with post natal depression, but I also found so much comfort and I could be in tears interviewing those real mums' stories and emotionally relating to them. I also strongly believe it is the Lord who brought those mums into my path and through so much prayer I recognised those mums are real mums out there who are also real heroes for Jesus. As I wrote their testimony and worked with them, I only had one vision that - through this huge collection of Real Mums' stories -

you as a reader will be delivered and will be touched deeply, emotionally, mentally and spiritually. You will truly know you are NOT ALONE in your motherhood journey and I promise you we really have a heavenly Father, JESUS CHRIST who loves you and cares for you and He gave you children knowing you can do this through His strength. Children are a blessing from the Lord and He wants us to treasure them with all our heart.

To my mum Lin Mei Lan who is now no longer with us I also want to dedicate this book. She and my father Chang Ching Hwa raised me up as a determined child and supported me all the way to this day! I am forever grateful. I also want to give a huge thank you to my husband Daniel and our miracle daughter Hannah, because both of you are the most precious gifts that I can have from the King Jesus. I love my husband and I love my dear daughter Hannah beyond words. I am forever grateful for all the support my husband and my daughter give me. My prayer is that there will be a domino effect from this book to all the readers, all the women around the globe, knowing that motherhood is hard on every level but still you are brave enough to carry the baby inside you and raise the child up and Jesus Christ will carry you through all the storms in your life.

The evidence reveals itself in those stories. Inside this book you will find real hardship, you will see real tears, you will relate to those real mums whose struggles are so vivid and my prayer is this, not only will you enjoy reading them, but also you will get deliverance and healing from these testimonies. Eventually I pray you will receive Jesus Christ into your heart as Lord and Saviour.

I personally almost gave up this book God put into my heart. Along my journey of motherhood I never wanted to have a child as I am HIV positive! Despite the odds Jesus let me experience a journey of HEALING. What a journey I have walked through those tough times and the healing journey with Jesus Christ. By writing the first story of myself, I decided to start interviewing mothers from different backgrounds and different nationalities. I purposely did it because this book is for all the women around the world. My hope is built on Jesus Christ and I believe the same Jesus Christ who helped me in dark times will also help you in your life's journey. Jesus is REAL in my life so I want you to discover Him for yourself. Jesus can help you - as long as you are willing to receive Jesus into your heart things will start to change. Even when we are faithless God is faithful.

I am deeply thankful to you who bought this book - either you know KoHsin personally or you are just curious about this book. I pray it will bring so much comfort and healing through those real mums' stories. I declare and prophesy over this book it will reach many women around the globe.

All of these mums have given me their consent and allowed me to write their testimony with their help and I am so thankful to each one of them.

Once again it's proven to me that when God gives you a vision, never give up on that vision. You need to carry on the vision until it comes to pass through the mighty Name of Jesus. It will take time to come to pass but still, NEVER GIVE UP. Let me repeat: NEVER GIVE UP.

It says in the Scripture:

"I can do all things through Jesus Christ who strengthens me." Mark 9 : 23.

Some mothers developed their love for their baby straight away! For some, the day they were born, there was the instant bond with their child because of breastfeeding, some were like me who suffered huge shock due to C section and slowly developed love towards my child Hannah. The most important thing is that true love from a mother is deep down in their heart and tremendously real. The sacrifice is so deep that motherhood is a process which, through labour and giving birth, transforms us from being a beautiful young woman into a mother! It's like the transformation from a caterpillar into a beautiful butterfly. After giving birth you pick yourself up, you recover and you learn to sacrifice for your newborn! You learn to make your child your first priority before you, it's a huge sacrifice. The protective instinct, the love, the effort you make to try to do the right thing for your children is always there. It is so hard trying to be a mother, no matter your culture or background, however it is alright to make mistakes – EVERYBODY DOES. It does not matter if it is a planned or unplanned child, in the end you realise the effort you put into your children brings out so much joy and love and makes motherhood so worthwhile. These real mums are everywhere and the struggles are so true as I found while writing those stories and a mother's love is so deep.

I am a born again Christian and I believe God gave me parenting responsibility. Being a mother is a learning process to love and protect and treasure your child. The love is there for your child every single day, forever, even when they grow up. You always love them and you put your children in your heart, always. I pray that you will love these stories as much as I do and I appreciate you spending time reading them. Thank you.

Recommendation from Annie Galloway.

I am so thankful for KoHsin and her courage to walk in His Spirit and Truth. Through the sharing of her testimony From HIV to Christ, and her prayers for God's healing to be done in my life I am Healed and receiving blessings from knowing KoHsin through God connections. Jesus has done Healing for myself and my family. KoHsin's authenticity, boldness and ability to speak Truth and Gospel are a gift from Jesus. It evident in the fruit of her works in writing, testifying and prayer. She is following the Lord, I can see in her love of her family and the people of God in different nations. Her dedication to writing this book to reach mothers out there and opening her heart to hearing the stories of the mothers is admirable. May the Lord continue to use her for His purpose and Glory. I am really thankful to know KoHsin and praying in agreement that this book will bring so much healing and minister to many women around the globe.

Recommendation from Mary Wu

I met KoHsin when I was doing missionary work related to the James Hudson Taylor Trail in Barnsley for two years from year 2013-2015. Our first encounter was during an overnight twenty-four hours prayer meeting at my apartment. That night, KoHsin shared with us her fears of becoming a mother after finding out she had HIV/AIDS, so we spent the evening comforting and praying for her health.

In 2016, I had moved back to Taiwan and when KoHsin was visiting, we got together with a group of ladies from Aglow International Republic of China (In Taiwan) and Aglow Ladies from Hong Kong to pray for her desires as well as God's will be done for her. Later on, when I found out that she was able to get pregnant and eventually I met her miracle daughter, Hannah, in Taiwan I was full of joy and thankfulness to God for His masterpiece! Hannah is so beautiful with bilingual features and certainly a blessing for the Lord to KoHsin's family.

I highly recommend reading this book "Real Mums Real Struggles Real Love and Real JESUS" which is a collection of over twenty Christian mothers' testimony about their struggles with motherhood and how Jesus helped them and transformed their lives. I know that, reading this book, the same Jesus will also transform your life too. I stand in prayers with KoHsin for this book to help and minister to many in Jesus' Name.

Recommendation from Kat Crawford

The first time I heard KoHsin's Testimony it was amazing, it encouraged me so much as a Christian. So I want to tell you that you did Not pick up this book by accident. I believe this is a divine appointment for you to read this book. The stories in this book clearly show the faithfulness of a loving and living Heavenly Father we have. A Heavenly Father that helped those mums will do the same for you. Thank you so much for KoHsin for reaching out to me and putting this book all together. She is an amazing passionate women of God. I believe many lives will be touched Amen.

Recommendation from Gloria Connally , Head of In Christ Service Outreach Ministry, USA.

I met KoHsin Illingworth in 2020 through a five days writing challenge workshop online. This workshop was for women of Christian faith who wanted to write a book from their heart. During the workshop she shared her testimony how she contracted HIV and how God met her in person and took her on a journey of healing and how she finally had a miracle child Hannah who is not infected with the HIV virus. People who joined the workshop were all amazed with her testimony. I also gave my personal testimony, how my life changed and my conversion to Jesus Christ. Then KoHsin sent me a friend request from Facebook and we began our communication through phone calls and Messenger. We began to pray for one another during the pandemic and I decided to start covering KoHsin and her ministry in prayer as I started to watch and follow KoHsin as GOD is opening doors for her.

Through KoHsin's testimony many people get encouraged to know Jesus. We became very close and she asked me to be part of this book on motherhood she was writing. God has shown me her heart, why she wants to write this book to minister to women. I agreed to submit the version of my testimony as a single mother, raising three young children sometimes only with the help of God. This book reveals the very issue of hardship of motherhood and how Jesus helped those mothers in the journey of parenting. After several months engaging with KoHsin and watching her develop a heart for helping mums who really struggle, I believe in KoHsin's vision and in this book. My ministry in the USA is certainly covering KoHsin in prayer for her to step out in faith boldly in everything she does for her Healed In Victory Ministry. I am so humble and happy my testimony is included in this book and I wholeheartedly recommend this book "Real Mums Real Struggles, Real Love Real Jesus". All the best to you KoHsin and keep soaring High for Jesus.

Mary Sue, Age 50, Born-again Christian – British. Pastor's wife at Gateway Church, Barnsley

I was born in the beautiful seaside town of St Ives in Cornwall, a few minutes' walk from several golden beaches. I was the youngest of four children, and the only girl. My Mum was delighted to finally have a little girl, but soon discovered that 'she'd rather have boy triplets than another maid' as she said frequently in her broad Cornish accent! My Mum was a Christian as was her mother, and we were brought up and raised in the Methodist Church, attending regularly, sometimes two to three times on a Sunday. My Dad was not a Christian; my Mum was backslidden when she met him, but returned to the Lord when I was about five years old. My Dad allowed us to go to Church and was not negative about it. He was thirty-two years older than my Mum, and when I hear people say that age doesn't matter if you love each other, I have to say that sadly it does, as the age gap can be too wide. It wasn't a happy marriage, but we were loved, although my Dad died suddenly when I was thirteen years old when he was eighty-two. My Mum was widowed at fifty and life was a struggle for us financially, but we knew the Lord's help and provision.

I gave my life to Jesus when I was twelve years old. I attended a Scripture Union youth camp, and the speaker at our nightly services invited us to give our lives to Jesus. Everything I had learnt in Sunday School and church clicked into place and I decided to follow Jesus there and then. I have continued to follow Jesus since that decision, and feel so privileged to have known the Lord my whole life. My passion now is to teach children about Jesus, and to plant seeds in their life so they too can know him.

When I left school I trained as a Secretary, then worked for the NHS as a Medical Secretary to a Hand

Surgeon for several years. However, at twenty-two I became restless as I had already reached as high as I could within the NHS at that time, and I also wanted to see something of the world. After much prayer, I decided to become an au pair in the USA. I prayed that if the Lord didn't want me to go, then He would close the door to it, and open the way He wanted me to go. As it was, the Lord opened the door and I went to Atlanta, Georgia for one year. This was a very tough year, as I was very homesick and missed my Mum in particular, as I was very close to her. However, the Lord was with me and strengthened me, and brought some wonderful Christian people into my life who helped me through. At one very down point, I heard the Lord audibly tell me to be patient. During that year I attended a Baptist Church and during a convention on 'leadership', I felt that God was calling me to Bible College - Church Leadership – and that I would be married to a Pastor.

The following year I went to Bible College, the year after that I led a team of young people on a year-long Church Planting mission, called a 'Seed Team'. At our first prayer meeting, I met Mark, my future husband! We became engaged on my twenty-fifth Birthday the following year and married the year after that. My husband was called to become a Methodist Minister and we moved to Bristol to begin his three year training programme. So the Lord completed his 'calling' to me when I became a Pastor's wife after Mark finished his training. We have now been involved in Ministry for twenty-six years, leaving the Methodist Church to be obedient to God's call on us to 'plant' a new church, called Gateway, which is now in its tenth year. I have supported my husband's ministry through this time, and my focus now is on children's ministry and ensuring they hear the Good News of Jesus whilst they are young.

During our time at Wesley College in Bristol, I became pregnant with our first child. I had a good and healthy pregnancy, taking exercise each day and eating healthily to ensure our firstborn had the best start in life. My due date came and went, and then started the labour which lasted for four days! The medics called it 'false labour', but it wasn't very false to me! The contractions were apparently Braxton Hicks contractions, which are practice ones, and should not be painful. However, unfortunately for me they were very painful, but as they weren't close enough together I wasn't allowed into hospital, and sadly the hospital wasn't very supportive. Having started contractions in the early hours of Saturday morning, our firstborn son Silas, was born at tea time by Ventouse delivery the following Tuesday. Ventouse is where they put a plastic cap over the baby's head to suck the child out, due to maternal exhaustion. I was twenty-nine years old and traumatised by the whole saga. Whilst in labour, the baby turned his body so his back was to my spine, and I am told it is one of the most painful forms of labour. Even though I had a long and difficult labour and delivery, I knew that the Lord's hand was upon me and I was thankful for a safe and healthy baby boy.

As we lived in flats at college in a communal block, we had many friends who all shared the same experiences as us. There were five of us all pregnant together, having our babies within six months of each other, and the support network and friendship was wonderful. However, one of my closest friends at the time had three children and was pregnant with her fourth, and was very forceful in her own opinions about pregnancy and childbirth. She told me in no uncertain times not to have an epidural form of pain relief as there were far too many risks, and so whilst in labour for so long, I was offered on several occasions an epidural, which because of my friend's advice I refused. This I believe, added to the trauma of my delivery, and with hindsight, I really should have had one. Imagine my disgust when she told me that she had had an epidural when she gave birth two months after me! Subsequently, I did warn my friend not to give such advice in the future. Indeed, I have said to many pregnant women since – everyone feels pain differently, everyone has a different way of coping and a different delivery. I recommend never to tell a pregnant woman what to and what not to do during labour, she must decide herself under the guidance of her own medical team! My friend apologised to me, and I have been able to forgive her despite my initial anger.

When Mark and I were first married and discussed the possibility of having children, we both decided that I would become full-time Mum to them and not return to paid employment, until we felt that the time was right. I felt strongly, and thankfully my husband agreed with me, that there was no point in having children for someone else to look after and see all the stages of development that I wanted to see and experience. Neither did we see the point in me working to then pay someone else to look after our children! Although our finances at times have been difficult, the Lord has been faithful to us and provided as our 'Jehovah Jireh'.

Silas was a delight to us and our families, and we were thrilled with our precious new gift from God. However, he was a difficult and demanding baby, crying a lot for the first three months of his life. I did my best to breastfeed, but found this very difficult, although I did manage twelve weeks to give my baby the best start in life. We were never really sure of his reasons for crying, whether he had wind, was hungry or had a sore head from his Ventouse delivery - he did have a cone shaped head for a while! I am so thankful to the Lord for my wonderful husband who was there to help as much as he could, never being afraid or bothered about changing nappies, taking him for rides in the car to settle his crying, and all sorts of little things to make life a bit easier for me. We were blessed though that he was a great sleeper, and slept through the night from six weeks. We could cope much better after a good night's sleep!

After my prolonged labour with Silas I felt for a couple of years that I wouldn't be able to face childbirth again, but slowly the longing for another child was there, and we were thankful to be blessed with a baby girl when Silas was three years old. My labour and delivery was much quicker, and our sweet little Grace was a much quieter and easier baby to cope with! However, we both had the sense that our family was not yet complete, and nearly three years later along came baby Samuel, this time with an even shorter labour and delivery. Baby Samuel had two big siblings to help love and nurture him, and Grace turned into his second mother, always looking after and loving her new baby. After him, we knew that our family was complete and he would be our last child. By then I was nearly thirty-six and felt that my body probably couldn't take any more pregnancies!

The Lord has truly blessed us as a family and we are so thankful for our beautiful children, two of whom are now adults and making their own way in the world. We believe that we have given them a strong foundation to build on, although we are not perfect and have failed at times as parents, our prayer for them is that throughout their lives they take hold of all the truths about Jesus that we have taught them over the years, and follow and serve Him as their Lord and Saviour. Some people say that being a full-time stay at home Mum is a sacrifice, but for us it has been the right thing for us to do. This has also enabled me to support Mark in his ministry, be there for him and our children without employers owning my time. I am so thankful to God for allowing us the privilege of being parents to three wonderful young people.

Phil. 4,13

"I can do all things through Christ who strengthens me."

Psalm 51, 10-12

"Create in me a pure heart, O God, and renew a steadfast spirit within me. Do not cast me from your presence or take your Holy Spirit from me. Restore to me the joy of your salvation and grant me a willing spirit, to sustain me."

Gloria Connally. Age 67, Born Again Christian. African American. Gospel singer

My name is Gloria Connally. I am a born again follower of Christ Jesus, born on May 6, 1953, now sixty-seven years old. I was born in the United States of America as an African American woman, who is now a mother, grandmother and great grandmother. God had a plan for me from the beginning, and He still does.

Jeremiah 29:11
"For I know the plans I have for you, declares the Lord, plans to prosper you and not to harm you, plans to give you hope and a future."

I did not realize when I left for college at eighteen years old, after leaving high school, that God had plans for my life that were totally polar to what I had planned for myself. My first time moving away from home, Cincinnati, Ohio, I found myself pregnant in my freshman year of college. I was totally unprepared for life, especially raising a baby as a single mother; I was still a child myself. Forced to leave school and campus, to go back home and try to work things through; to care for my child and myself. I ended up moving back closer to campus several months after my child was born, with the hopes of completing my education, acquiring a stable career and becoming self-sufficient. Things did not work out as I had planned and once again I had to move back home. For several years I was in and out of colleges and universities and worked several jobs in between to provide for my child alone.

While on my journey, I found myself involved with taking drugs, mostly prescribed in the beginning, then I began taking street drugs and drinking alcohol. I was trying to medicate myself by numbing the tremendous pain I was experiencing physically, emotionally, mentally, with no spiritual life to speak of, though I grew up "in church." After several years of struggling through this life, I met a man in June of 1979, a few months before I committed my life to Jesus Christ and became Holy Spirit filled on September 7, 1979. Shortly after meeting him, I had overdosed from drugs and alcohol and found myself in the emergency room fighting for my life.

The doctors did not think I would pull through, but God had a different plan for me. As I was lying there dying in the hospital bed, I had an encounter with Jesus. I saw my life pass slowly in front of me in slow motion like it was on a movie screen moving sideways and it sickened me. I cried out and said, "I'm sorry!" then I went unconscious. After several hours I regained consciousness. My vital signs became stable and there was no sign of anything being wrong with me. I knew Jesus had saved my life. I was released from the hospital and the next day I went back to work. I looked for my friend that had been asking me to attend bible study with her. I asked her if I could go with her that very evening. We went and I accepted Jesus as my Lord and Savior and I was baptized and filled with the Holy Spirit.

I and the man I had met in June got married and had two living children together. It was a very poor and wrong decision on my part but God still had a plan for my life. After several years of a very difficult marriage, I was serving God but my husband was not. It was during the turbulent years that God showed me who He really was, is, and forever will be. In fact me, my husband and my children were living in a tent for three weeks, that how bad it was.

When my husband finally divorced me, after several years of him living with another woman, I learned first hand that Daddy God is my provider, protector, healer, deliverer, restorer and everything else I need, especially in the raising of my children. When I got so sick and could not work, He provided us with shelter, food, clothing, protection and everything I was trying to do on my own. I had no income and nothing and no one but relied on Jesus. I was a single mom, so we were homeless and I had no money - that was the worst part of my chapter. I am so thankful I learned to pray, I was a Christian then. Later on my children never knew we were homeless until I gave my testimony one day at the church. My oldest son said as a boy he thought mommy was taking them camping and with a little food we survived. Jesus provided everything and I started to teach my children how to pray for everything.

One Thanksgiving holiday we were down to our last meal and I called all my children into the kitchen and I had all of us lay our hands on the refrigerator and our cabinets in the kitchen because they were complete empty. I prayed out loud to Jesus, thanking God He will provide for my family and we will have a Thanksgiving meal. Then we just began to worship and praise God for what He is going to do for my family. Later on in the evening suddenly there was a knock on the door. One of my church members, who in fact know nothing about our financial situation, felt that God told him to come to help my family! He had come with many bags of groceries and it filled the entire freezer and refrigerator and we had such a great Thanksgiving meal with my church friend. There was so much food for all my family plus enough to bless my neighbour as well. I had many testimonies like this so now I trust the Lord as JEHOVA JIREH. He is my provider and He is sufficient for me and my child so I can honestly tell you everyone else called upon His Holy name.

I had very little outside support during this time. Daddy God truly taught me who He was. I raised my children with the loving care of God the father, through Jesus Christ His son and the power of the Holy Spirit. I trained them up in the way they should go. I called on Him for help.Every day I prayed. Matthew 6:, especially verses 31 and 33 and it says:

"therefore take no thought saying what shall we eat or what shall we drink or wherewithal shall we be clothed?" "For after all these things do the gentiles seek, for your heavenly father knows that you need of all these things. But seek ye first the kingdom of God and His righteousness and all these things shall added unto you."

I would not been able to survive and live through those perilous years without knowing God was there to help me care for my children. As they grew in their teenage years they strayed away from the things of God because of a lot of hurt and circumstances that were beyond any of our control, but I am watching Him bring His prodigal children back home to Him. They all have a firm and solid foundation of teachings from His holy word and they are now putting those very same scriptures and spiritual principles before God to use as they raise their own children, as single parents. I have always taught them that God says, try me and see If these things be true. They are finding out for themselves that they are true. I give Daddy God praise forever for the plan He has for me coming into fruition, for I have tried Him and He is faithful. I stand on His promise,

Lamentations 3:22 and 23.
"The steadfast love of the Lord never ceases, His mercies never come to an end; they are new every morning; Great is thy faithfulness! " Amen.

Maria, age 35,
Slovakian, Christian

I am from Slovakia and I moved to the United Kingdom only few years ago. I am willing to let this interview to go on even though my English was not good and I thank KoHsin for being willing to listen and write down my story. I was only twenty years old when I found out I was pregnant. At the time my man was only my boyfriend, I loved him and I wanted to have a baby with him! As simple as that. I had an easy pregnancy, but I remember the date my baby boy was born, I remember clearly, it was an annual holiday in my country and the doctor who attended me kept saying "You keep push quick quick! Because I need to go home". I will always remember that, because the doctor just wanted to go home and leave me alone to give birth. It was such an irresponsible doctor.

I had a big baby boy. I had forceps with him and for two weeks I couldn't walk properly and was trying to recover. The first struggle was that in my country the health system was not good. There was no midwife or health visitor to teach you, so I have no idea how to be a mother. I was also very young. My husband works hard, however we were really struggling with money. I remember sometimes I have to starve myself to buy milk and nappies for the baby. I am a very fertile women, so later I found out quickly I was pregnant again! I remember I came home, told my husband I was pregnant again and I had mixed feelings. Still in my country it's not legal to get an abortion at all. You need to have a proper reason why you want to get rid of a baby. My husband told me we will try to survive and he will support my decision, no matter what, so I had my second child.

We moved to the UK as a result of human trafficking. My husband came to the UK first and later I came because I was at first very scared to leave my country which I feel so comfortable with. However I know I love my husband and my children need their father and we need to be somewhere as a family so we moved to Bradford. It was a very stressful time that we don't have much money, all of us staying in one room only, a small space and we try to survive. Then I found out I am pregnant again! I remember I had a blood test and also when I found out I am pregnant the third time I was in such shock and so scared because our finance was a disaster and we really struggled.

However I know deep down the NHS system here is good and I prayed and decided to have the third child. His name is Jacob and he certainly came as a shock, a nice surprise. I see all my three children, I love them so much. I don't have much money but I do borrow books from the library and I will read to them, love them, kiss them. I find it very hard because money is a struggle, however real struggle comes with not speaking proper English and trying to survive here, also complete lack of sleep! With looking after three children it is certainly a struggle, a daily struggle. Until now we five of us only live in a small apartment. The best thing my husband did is that he had the vasectomy operation. He makes sure we will not have any more children again. Because I also found out something is not right with my cervix at the smear test we try not to have sex as often as possible. I love all my three children to the moon and back and I will do everything to protect them and raise them. We don't have much money at all however I know I will always try to be as good a mother as I can be. I am now really thanking God for everything I have, the family I have, and also thanking God for bringing me a better life and providing for me in the time of need.

Dawn Gould,
Born again Christian, British.

Isaiah 40 : 31
"Those who wait on the Lord, He will renew their strength they will soar on wings like eagles. They will run and not grow weary, they will walk and not be faint."

I was brought up in a broken home, both parents relied on government benefits. Some Christmases, we didn't have presents at all. One Christmas we only had pancakes, that's how bad it was. I remember many times we actually went round the back of Morrisons' warehouse in the car park where they put the out of date food. We needed to pick up that out of date food for my family's survival. My dad was on benefits and he used to sell the things in the house. For example he would sell the TV and get the money and then go straight away to the pub. My dad was an alcoholic and had depression. There was always argument in my house, they would swear at each other or hit each other. My mum found it hard to look after us. I was told later on that my mum used to put me in a Moses basket in my pram and put me as a baby outside the back door for a few hours , which was supposed be a good thing back then. She would feed me, as I remember, but she struggled financially and mentally to look after me properly. Now when I look back over my childhood there is a lot of rejection in my life, because I feel that maybe I wasn't supposed to be born, so I felt totally neglected and unwanted as a child. I had no bonding with my parents.

I started going to school but I didn't do well. When they did a spelling test on me I failed and the school system told me I was thick. Years later I found out that I had dyslexia and I needed to have extra support from school. When I was a child I used to love going to school so much because things were so bad at home. My parents were not even bothered if I had any education or not. I loved going to school and seeing my teachers every day because it was better than staying home.

I was sexually abused when I was young. In later years when I went to church, one day the Holy Spirit told this member of the church to minister to me and the Lord revealed so clearly to this person that, when I was a child, strangers and my dad's drunken buddies and one of my family members actually came into the house regularly and tried to force sex on me. I used to love to go to one of my family member's house to play but I knew something was not right as I knew I was certainly being sexually abused by different men. Because it happened at such a young age, some of these memories are totally blurred because I couldn't remember. Still the Lord showed me when I got older, thank you Jesus. As a result, I became very ruthless and angry and I turned out to be a tomboy. I became like a person to whom sex means nothing but deep down I was really desperately seeking love. At the time I didn't even know there is a God in heaven who loves me. There was a lady I encountered who told me about the gospel but I swore at this lady with the 'F' word as I didn't believe her.

Then I moved to Cornwall with my partner but later on he ended up in prison so I became a single mum. There was a lady called Mary who decided to start talking to me and look after me and my baby. She is an angel who took us under her wings, and when I walked into Mary's house there was a strong sense of warmth and I know I can feel a sense of peace and there are Bible scriptures on the wall and pictures of Jesus on the wall. As I went into the room, I could feel a strong sense of warmth, of presence, of knowing someone was there. Later on I found out it was the presence of God, so I started asking them what this meant. I asked her question upon question about scriptures and Jesus. At the time I thought Jesus was only to do with Easter and Christmas and it meant nothing to me, but that day I started asking questions. Two weeks later I said to Mary "You are going to church on Sunday, right? I am coming with you! I want to see if the Jesus you are on about is real!" So I started going to church with my son, with Mary, and something drew me to want to go to church. After one month there was a healing meeting at the church in Cornwall and I decided to go. Thankfully my friend's son looked after my baby boy so I could go to this healing meeting. I was struggling to understand because of my learning difficulties, but I remember by the end of the meeting I was so amazed that I had my hands in the air and I decided to give my life to Jesus!

The best way to describe me around that time of my life is I was a cocoon with a hard shell. I was so broken inside in every way and I was damaged, I decided no one can hurt me, so I put a tough face on, but inside of me is very soft and needs love and God knows that. He knows I need His love and I thank God that this lady Mary, who sadly died, was the first person to lead me to Jesus and I am forever grateful. I really felt the presence of God's love at Mary's house. When I got my first Bible God performed a miracle. At first I couldn't even read the Bible because of my dyslexia but I did have the hunger for God's love and slowly God is teaching me how to read the Bible. As I was reading the Bible sentence by sentence I slowly to learned how to write and read also! I can honestly tell you now I am so amazed I can read the Bible, even though people told me I was thick. God really has done miracles inside me.

One of the supernatural healings I had was when I was bleeding and I was in so much pain and then I went a church meeting where the Minister that day was preaching

Mark 5 : 25.
"And a women was there who had been subject to bleeding for twelve years. She had suffered a great deal under the care of many doctors and had spent all she had. But instead of getting better, she grew worse. When she heard about Jesus she came up behind him in the crowd and touched his garment because she thought 'If I just touch his clothes I will be healed.' Immediately the bleeding stopped and she felt in her body and she was freed from her suffering. "

I remember so well, during that time, when the pain in my womb was so bad I couldn't even go to church. That day, when I heard this Bible message, I went to the front for the prayer and the minister prayed over me. I remember being prayed over and I do believe the healing took place for me inside my body so the pain and the bleeding completely stopped. That day I truly experienced supernatural healing from Jesus. Glory to GOD.

The healing process kept going slowly as the Minister in Cornwall taught us to write down on a piece of paper the names of the men who abused me and then I had to say the forgiveness prayer and throw the piece of paper into the bin. There were so many men who abused me in my past, most of them forced themselves on me. I can honestly say I was sexually abused badly and it affected me mentally. I had to go through this process of learning to forgive and I realised I must forgive all of them in order to continue the walk with God. I know God is so real but I did go through this painful process. Every time when I said the forgiveness prayer I was so amazed, there was a huge sense of release in my body as the presence of the Lord was doing its work inside of me. I felt my pain being lifted up and there was a release and I gave to God. Through the forgiveness prayer I forgave myself and I forgave those men. Some of the memories are so many years back. Still I managed to forgive all of them.

I have four children today, the first two with my first husband who was so violent I got to the point I couldn't take it anymore so we got divorced. My second husband left me and did not take on any responsibility either. So as I can recall I was a single mum even when I was married. In my motherhood journey sometimes I struggled so with money and I learned to pray to God constantly that my children needed clothes and food. When I prayed, usually a few days later people would just give me food and second hand clothes. God is so faithful and when I look back, I really did have the things I needed for my children. Thank you Lord.

I also struggled with post-natal depression and learning difficulty and I am so thankful that my church friends took me out and prayed with me and lifted up my spirits, and helped me out and so after six months I just felt better deep down. Because my own parents had no sense of responsibility, they didn't take care of me, so today I decided I wanted to be a different mum for my children and thank you Jesus for helping me. I know I recovered from my post-natal depression. Even though I had a husband, he didn't do anything for me or help me with parenting and I can really say that being a single mum is so hard. I am amazed, every time when I prayed for what I needed for my family God did provide and I never ended up homeless.

Now I am a born again Christian. Because of my learning difficulty I truly thank God that I met KoHsin and she helped me to put my testimony in order. I have had many men let me down in the past but God is so faithful and God never lets me down. God performed miracles inside me - I couldn't read at all due to my poor education background but now I can read my Bible and I can read scriptures. God also did a miracle in me as I don't feel rejected and useless any more. I am now seeking God and I pray my testimony will help you to want to seek Jesus.

Romans 12:2

"Do not conform to the pattern of this world, but be transformed by the renewing of your mind. Then you will be able to test and approve what God's will is, his good pleasing and perfect will ."

Kat Crawford, Age 38,
Born again Christian, American. Worship leader at Arise Church, Louisiana

Psalms 27:4 -6.

"One thing I ask of the Lord, this is what I seek, that I may dwell in the house of the Lord all the days of my life, to gaze upon the beauty of the Lord and to seek Him in His temple. For in the days of trouble He will keep me safe in his dwelling. He will hide me in the shelter of His tabernacle and set me high upon a rock. Then my head will be exalted above the enemies who surround me; at His tabernacle will I sacrifice with shouts of joy. I will sing and make music to the Lord. "

My life has taken a lot of twists and turns. Growing up I lived with one of my brothers, my Dad and my Grandparents. I had been to church but it was not something we did regularly. I had even been baptized when I was a child but looking back I am not sure I knew I was doing it, just that I was searching for something. When I was twelve my father passed away suddenly so I lived with his sister, my aunt, who was abusive to me. Through a series of difficult events, I ended up running away and being put into the state's foster care system. I moved from house to house, mainly because that is often how the foster system works. It wasn't until the state found my mother that there was an option for me to move across country and live with her.

When I moved to Louisiana my brother had already been living with her a short while. She was saved by God and went to church but I was not really interested in that side of things. I hung out with friends, partied and did what most teenagers did in a small country town. It wasn't until one of my friends passed away in a bad car accident that I really took a hard look at the direction I was going.

That day I gave my life to Jesus Christ, but I still didn't know what that actually meant. I had to learn what a saved life was because, even though I had a mother that went to church, she didn't teach me that. About two months after I got saved I found out I was pregnant. At age seventeen I didn't think my life was over but I sure was willing to take on the task of raising a child. I knew that I wanted to be responsible and chose to keep my beautiful daughter, who is now twenty years old.

After I had my daughter I went on to get married, to be involved in worship at my church and have two more beautiful daughters. When I was pregnant with my third daughter, we found out that there were complications that the doctors believed would keep me from carrying her to full term. I prayed but I cannot say that I wasn't concerned. I wondered, God, you are her healer I believe you are the best healer, Jesus you can heal, I am going to believe in you no matter how this turns out.

I had my daughter at thirty-seven weeks and she was taken by an airplane to a children's hospital one state over! I had to travel four hours driving to be able to get to her after I gave birth. The day after she was born she went into surgery that lasted a total of eleven hours! I was not able to be there yet since I was recovering from a C section. All I could do that day was pray to Jesus and trust the Lord to be in the operation room for her. My husband was with her and I was so glad that he was there for her. While I was pregnant the third time the Lord told me her name was Hope, and that is what we decided to name her.

Hope is now eleven years old. We have been through countless surgeries, hospital stays and doctors' visits. We have been told that she would not do several things that other kids can do but I have personally watched miracles after miracles unfold in front of my eyes as God has faithfully continued to show Himself mighty powerfully in her life and ours!

Has it been easy? No. Not at all. Have I wondered what it might look like if this wasn't the road I was on? Yes. Has it been worth it? The answer is YES. Honestly, I don't believe I could have been through what I have been through and not have the Lord by my side holding my hand and carrying me through! I have experienced His love, and His faithfulness and provision have guided me through countless twists and turns.

GOD IS FAITHFUL. There is no other way to put it. He reveals His goodness every time when I now look at my three girls. Megan the oldest, Lilian my second and Hope my third.

There is one interesting fact that I found out after I had Hope. I did not look up what her name really meant until after she was born but 'Hope' means 'confident expectation' so, before I even knew everything she would go through, God was actually saying to me to have a confident expectation that she will not only survive, but thrive. I believe that God has that in mind for all of His children who trust Him. Today I am so thankful that I can truly say I am His daughter and He loves me that much and died for me on the cross. I have truly experienced His love and His miracles and His goodness.

Thank you Jesus. Today I serve as a worship leader at my church also I have been writing songs singing and I make music for the Lord. I pray as my testimony will touch your heart and I thank KoHsin with many conversations that I believe KoHsin's vision is fantastic as this book will minister and help many women.

Revelation 19: 10

"At this I fell at his feet to worship him but he
said to me. Do not do it! I am a fellow servant with you
and with your brothers who hold to the testimony of
Jesus. Worship GOD! For the testimony of Jesus is the
spirit of prophecy. "

Anna Israel, Age 45,
Born again Christian, Nigerian.

I was born in a very, very poor background. My parents are both Christians and they are farmers, they own land and grow vegetables. My dad left the village for a while and that is when he met my mum and they got married at church. When I came to the world my parents had already buried five babies because in my country a child can die during childbirth. I was the sixth of my family and because my mum had buried so many dead she decided to send me to missionaries for them to raise me up. In my childhood memories I always remember growing up at church. Every day I would go to church to learn from the missionaries. They would pick me up and play with us and teach us how to read and my parents were very happy I was there.

When I got a bit older the missionaries asked me to go with them as I only had primary education and we moved to another city with them. I decided to go with them and they set up a Bible school and a secretary school for me and I helped with their household. I cleaned their house and I stayed with them and I went to Bible school and learned all the skills.

When I was twenty years old I met my husband Israel and we got married at church. For the first two years I did take contraception pills and later on I got pregnant. In fact I had a very good pregnancy. When I gave birth to my son I had to be induced and the baby was late and the doctors performed a C section.

When my baby son was nine months old he started being unable to walk and couldn't breathe and had very bad fever. The next thing I knew the baby was collapsing in my arms and I went to the doctors at the hospital and by then my baby son literally died in my arms. He had no breath at all. Because my faith is so strong I decided not to take my baby to the bigger hospital. I instantly took my baby to the church. People heard me crying and many people followed me to the church and began praying. The whole church was praying over my child to bring life back to him. By then the elders were breathing into the baby and many people were praying in tongues and praying over life, over death, for the baby. The baby came back to life! At this point I broke the curse of my family because my family have had many baby deaths and I really believe God will give me children. I also know God can do anything.

After a few hours praying more and more people were coming into the church praying for the child. As I mentioned I live in a small village and God performed a big miracle so that my baby came back to life! When I look on back this I can only say it's a miracle. God not only let me but the whole village experience this miracle. Later I dedicated my child to the altar and we had a proper naming and dedication service.

I had two healthy sons. When I was pregnant with my third baby, one night I had a bad dream. A women came into the dream and wanted to give me a gift and I knew it felt uncomfortable and I had a proper spiritual attack and I knew in my heart the woman in my dream is a real witch from the devil. I was five months pregnant at this time and the next day when I awoke my mind was so disturbed and I couldn't sleep and I couldn't eat and I was really suffering and my baby was inside me jumping up and down. I knew my baby was disturbed also. I knew something was wrong and the baby could die because I was mentally so disturbed and my baby was disturbed so I knew it's a spiritual attack and it's from the dark evil so I immediately went to church asking for help! This was the hardest time of my life, because I needed to leave my boys at home with my mum to look after them while I was at church by myself. I was living inside the church and it's not easy, the church didn't have resources.

But I did have people come to church to look after me and bring me food or comfort and finally I delivered my third child inside the church. I delivered the baby with the strength from the Lord, that is the time I know it's only me and God. Sometimes on our journey it's really just you and God and it was a very tough time but I thank God I survived and I now have four children who are all healthy.

I can honestly tell you how many times I have seen miracles in my life. Because of how I was brought up in a very poor family, even my parents had crises in their faith just because they had to bury so many dead children. So they can see how I overcame difficulty through my faith. Now I am a born again Christian and I can tell you there is nothing God cannot do. I now have strong faith because of everything I have been through and every time when I can't find a way to survive, I always see that God provides our needs. Even when my husband and myself lost our jobs, God still provided and in many ways I can really say all my children are miracles, they let me carry on, and I need to trust God because God trusts me. He entrusts to us the responsibility of bringing up the children and now my children love going to church with me. Now I serve the Lord with all my heart and I am also a missionary.

In my life experience, problems come in so many ways, but God's Grace kept me going all these years. Since I came to know Jesus Christ He has been so faithful to me and my family. I have learned to always put God first and God never lets me down. I want to tell you that our God is not the last hope but He is the ONLY hope in times of trouble. In every trouble and every trial God can carry you through the storm so don't give up because God is with you.

I'm thankful that KoHsin helped me write down my testimony. Honestly I truly experienced, exactly like how Jesus brought Lazarus back to life, so He brought my baby boy from death to life. Many witnesses in my village experienced that miracle that day when they saw how my baby boy came back to life from death. I just want to tell you Jesus is the miracle worker and He has the power to perform miracles in your life and all you need to do is to TRUST HIM.

Proverbs 22.2.

"Rich and poor have this in common, the Lord is the maker of them all."

Psalm 72 18-19.

"Praise be to the lord God, the God of Israel who alone does marvellous deeds. Praise be to His glorious name forever, may the whole earth be filled with His glory, amen and amen."

KoHsin Illingworth, Taiwanese, Born again Christian. Director of Healed In Victory Ministry

Thank you Jesus for blessing me more than I deserve!

I was brought up in a good home in Taiwan, a busy district called Yong Ho district where my parents both worked hard in the First Commercial Bank. I was told to be a good girl, to study hard and also I was an insecure child when I was young. I was always trying to achieve good grades in my studies and when I look back I realise I wanted to please my parents. I am so thankful to my mum to this day, she let me learn piano lessons when I was young so I developed an interest and musical talent when I was a young kid. I am still able to play piano today and sing because I love music and I am grateful for my parents as they worked really hard for me to receive a good education.

I walked into a church at the age of fifteen and I decided to get baptised when I was eighteen, since then I knew Jesus has a plan and by the grace of GOD I enrolled into Christ College to study Mass Communication because I wanted to be a journalist. Later on I graduated with good Honours and then studied harder and I came to the United Kingdom in 2004 to study a Master's degree in journalism. While I was studying as an international student I was invited to a Christmas party in a hotel and unfortunately I ended up being raped in a hotel room. My body was hurt and I also felt broken and I waited until the man passed out on the bed so I could run out of the hotel that night.

After the rape, I forced myself to go back to studying and I thank God I finally finished my studies. The rape was a trauma and the Lord healed me later on.

I am very grateful that I met my British husband in 2006 and we fell in love and decided to get married. We got married in a beautiful Yorkshire hotel and then we went to Italy for our honeymoon. Unfortunately, after a year I started having erratic behaviour and depression so, sadly, after a while my family had to section me into a mental facility. I remember I prayed to GOD and I survived inside the mental hospital. After being discharged, one day I completely collapsed at home and ended up in an ambulance and by the time I got to hospital I was seriously ill. When I awoke in the hospital bed the doctor told me I was dying with millions of HIV virus inside my body and I was in a very critical condition in danger of dying with AIDS. So thank GOD, today when I look back to this day, God's timing was never wrong. He knew I wouldn't be able to survive for another week so God allowed me to end up in hospital being taken care of by the medical professionals.

While I was dying with HIV I received so much medication and I had suicidal thoughts. Still there were angels to help me. I knew it because JESUS didn't let me die and He allowed me to recover! My husband is my angel and I am so grateful for the doctors' care. Psalm 23, verse 4 says:

"Even though I walk through the valley of the shadow of death, I will fear no evil, for you are with me your rod and your staff they comfort me .

I certainly walked through the Valley of Death as there were millions of HIV virus already spreading massively all through my body and I almost died! By the grace of GOD I am alive today, so thank you Jesus! Thank you Jesus, you have saved my life so today I can be alive and be a witness for you.

After staying in the HIV isolation ward for almost six months, I was finally allowed to go home and one day I heard the Voice of GOD calling me. The voice was saying "KoHsin I am waiting for you, KoHsin I am waiting for you, come back to me. At first I looked around but there was nobody in the room, then later I knew the voice was from the Lord so I took a taxi to a local church. Then through the help of the local Baptist Church I decided to come back to Jesus as a Prodigal Daughter and learned to forgive myself and forgive the man who raped me.

Praying for forgiveness is very important because Jesus forgives all our sins. I started going to church regularly and thank you Lord for continuing to heal me spiritually and mentally. For almost six years, because I am HIV Positive and I am taking medication, so in the back of my mind I knew it was a huge risk for me to have a child. Still God really had a better plan! I received my first miracle when my HIV virus dropped down from twenty-two thousand to zero in a very short time. Then I continued to pray sincerely for the Lord to heal my body. The year of 2015 was significant as I saw the miracle as my virus dropped and I continued to pray daily. I went to Aglow National Conference in October and many Christian ladies prayed over me in a hotel room asking the Lord to open my womb so I could conceive a healthy child. A lady saw in a vision that I was going to have a beautiful baby girl. Then I conceived around Christmas 2015, thank you Lord.

I didn't have an easy pregnancy as I was still taking medication and they put me onto special care but I am so grateful for family and friends' help. Due to my age I was also finding it hard to work as an interpreter but by the grace of GOD I had a C section in August 2016 and I gave birth to Hannah.

Hannah is a Miracle child because, even despite the risk of infection, she was tested completely healthy and no trace of HIV virus in her little body! The consultant told me in her own words "Hannah is so small but so perfectly formed" that so moved my heart and I know it is the Lord blessing me with this child. Not only did the Lord allow me to recover from dying from AIDS He also healed my body step by step. I had such emotional mixed feelings when I gave birth to my child. I felt I had run a marathon during the pregnancy but after giving birth my body was bleeding and I was completely house-bound. The idea of having no clue how to look after a tiny baby plus still trying to recover was hard.

When I reached out to my Christian friends a few of them told me I should NOT complain. I should be thankful to God! Very soon I was diagnosed with Post Natal Depression and I found it so hard in the beginning. I also discovered I needed the assurance of knowing I was loved but when everyone was giving attention to my baby, I was jealous of my child! Because I was not in my right mind I knew I loved Hannah so much, but part of me felt she had taken over and I was feeling very neglected and thinking all the attention is on Hannah. Through counselling help and certainly seeking GOD and asking advice how to being a mum, I gradually learned how to be a mother! I remember I decided to go back to work as a Court interpreter by taking pain-killers in the court room break and I sent my baby to a child-minder for a while. That is how I could cope with my sanity, because the idea of looking after a baby twenty-four seven just made me more depressed and I am honestly very grateful for my family's support and help as we were both struggling and we overcame it together.

Before I conceived a baby I was struggling with the idea "How I can have a healthy child?" The Lord healed me by allowing me to have courage to move forward, then I finally conceived by praying more sincerely and that is when I realised God continued to heal me physically and bless me more than I deserve. Me and my husband could have had a HIV child with the risk involved but thanks be to GOD we have a healthy child.

During my pregnancy the Lord told me to called my child "Hannah." He gave me the scripture to comfort me during the pregnancy .

1 Samuel 1 verse 26 to 27
"As surely as you live my lord I am the women who stood here beside you praying to the Lord. I prayed sincerely for this child, and the Lord has granted me what I asked of him. So now I give him to the Lord. For his whole life he will be given over to the Lord."

According to the Scriptures, Hannah was finally granted the prayer; the Lord blessed Hannah with her son Samuel and she dedicated Samuel to the Lord. I felt exactly the same. I prayed to the Lord sincerely and God granted my prayer. I was a woman who was dying with AIDS and through a journey of healing from Jesus he blessed me with a healthy child that is more than I deserve.

Joshua 1 verse 9.
"Have I not commanded you? Be strong and courageous. Do not be terrified, do not be discouraged, for the Lord your God will be with you wherever you go."

<u>Annie Galloway, illustrator</u>

Proverbs 3 verses 5 -6
Trust in the Lord with all your heart and lean not
on your own understanding, in all your ways to
acknowledge Him and He will make your path straight.

For most of my life Jesus was not at the center guiding my choices and thoughts. I was born again at the age of forty-six and began reading the Bible. I was born in 1970 in the spring in a small city north of Chicago. As long as I can remember I always believed in God. My father was a college professor and my mother an elementary teacher. I am the youngest of three. Until the age of six I went to Quaker Meeting with my family and then we stopped going except for occasionally on Easter. I was very quiet and had difficulty speaking. I was deeply sensitive to how others felt including the anxiety and depression in my family. I was well behaved so I didn't draw attention to myself. This actually hindered me because I was really needing more help than I showed. I thought I needed to be perfect and it was very difficult for me to be corrected and to fail. I did not realize that I could come to my parents and teachers for guidance and support. This led to many problems for me as I entered into my teen years and adulthood.

I grew up believing Jesus is a good man and there is God. I was taught he lived a long time ago and was a human of justice and peace like Martin Luther King and Gandhi.In high school I went on a school trip to Greece and I was sexually assaulted while abroad. I didn't know who to talk to for support. The shame was unbearable. I thought I needed to be perfect and to have such an event happen to me I felt broken. I became victim minded. I turned to drugs and alcohol and to running away when anything would make me uncomfortable. In 1988 I started college and continued using drugs, having sex, by the end of my first year I was pregnant. My family was politically liberal and believed in Pro-Choice. I learned that to be a strong independent woman is to go to school and focus on a career. As a deeply empathetic young woman the thought of killing my first baby was something I couldn't wrap my mind around. I had the abortion. Afterwards my heart broke in a way - as a woman it was like my core of who I was to become a wife and a mother was taken from me. I was devastated and in this moment God was with me though I didn't have this understanding. I didn't process this grief with anyone I just pushed it down inside of me.

The cycle continued. I hid in alcohol, drugs and relationships that ended in the devastation of heartbreak and abortion. I began to believe that I was not worthy to be a wife or a mother. I didn't have any confidence in my identity as a woman. When I received my college diploma I was numb. I would go through the motions in my life with family and friends but inside I was experiencing so much confusion, insecurity and emotional pain. My sister was living in Philadelphia working at the Friends Center helping Quaker teens so I moved to Philadelphia to teach at a Friends School. I found a beautiful community and purpose in being a Quaker assistant teacher. I did not know that a school experience could be so deeply fulfilling. I began to seek healing in secular ways - psychotherapy, new age spirituality and in reading Self

Help books and other practices that "free" us from emotional pain and so I went around and around in circles seeking healing and peace. I had wonderful experiences in Quaker Sweat Lodge, boyfriends, meaningful work but still I was not settled and the wounds of my past continued to negatively influence my present. The shame would not lift, it was a heavy yoke to bear. I still didn't know that I could be saved, forgiven and restored by Jesus.

The first time Jesus revealed himself to me was at a Healing Conference and training in 1996. The teacher took us on a guided meditation. I closed my eyes and focused on visualizing the path... now walk through the meadow, finally you will come to a door... open the door. In my mind's eye I was at a cave and the door opened. I came inside and my grandmother was there. I turned and then I saw Jesus standing before me. I looked at him, I asked him, "Why are you here?" He said to me, "I am your teacher, I will teach you about healing and I will always be with you". This had a profound impact but I still was decades away from being born again.

I continued for many years in self-centered brokenness. I had many two to three year relationships but none led to marriage. I didn't stand up for my value because I didn't know my identity, my created value by God. I was adding up all the failures and weighing the pain. In 2000 I moved to Vermont. I worked at a non-profit for homeless people. Yet again I was heartbroken from a relationship that did not lead to marriage. I figured something was really wrong with me that I couldn't be in a relationship. I was convinced that I was unworthy to be a wife or a mother because of all the shame and fear of failing again. I became more bitter than ever before and additionally I was becoming desperate to have a baby. I was thirty-three years old. I was attending a Quaker Meeting in Vermont and had become friends with a man. I became pregnant out of wedlock and married a few months later. We weren't ready for marriage or to have a baby together.

I imagine going through these events with a family loving Jesus and having truth to walk in His strength and His Love. But Jesus tells us "don't look back" and He knows the course of our life, the steps we will take. He is always with us even when we don't know Him.

My husband was struggling with depression and I was pregnant and learning how to become a wife, finally, after so many years of failed relationships. I was impatient, bitter and discouraged from so many years of waiting to have my own family. I was not compassionate to my husband going through the trials of becoming a husband and father. We also had joyful moments but more often we did not walk in agreement on issues of family, faith and parenting. When our daughter was born was a wonderful day for our family but it was still shrouded in the wounds of the past and the challenges of a new marriage.

Our daughter was born in the spring of 2004. I was so overwhelmed and filled with so much joy to become a mother! Our midwife said to us your daughter has special needs. She had delivered hundreds of babies and had a sense that she was different. We could see early on that she was a sensitive child. She did not like to be held or touched and she was extremely sensitive to noise.

As she grew we saw her intelligence and sense of humor. She loved to laugh at books - she looked at books from when she was a month old. Her language was developed at a very young age. I was devoted to her and had difficulty balancing being a mother and a wife. I stayed home with her for the first four years and then I felt internal pressure and financial pressure that I needed to work. I had a dream in my heart to start a Quaker School in Vermont. I thought my daughter could grow up in this school and that would give her the security and understanding about the world that I didn't have growing up. Three years working on the school with an amazing Board of Directors and it was going to open with a few families, we had everything ready to go and the unexpected happened!

In the spring of 2010, my daughter began to develop seizures. They had started as night terrors and after receiving the MMR vaccination and she stopped having eye contact and responding verbally. I did not understand what was happening to our beautiful daughter. She was six years old; in a matter of months she went from a healthy joyful child to having forty to sixty seizures a day. The dream of going to the Quaker school was gone and we were thrown head first into a sea of medical terms, doctors, prescription drugs, tests, regular trips to the Emergency Department. It was the worst nightmare! I listened to the medical doctors, we traveled to three states and sought opinions from many neurologists. My daughter tried more than twenty pharmaceuticals, tests, different diets, everything we could think of that may reverse the seizures and let our girl heal and rest. They all said 'we don't know what else we can do for my daughter. She is very complicated, we have never seen a seizure disorder like this,' brain surgery wasn't an option. There was no hope left.

Early on in the process, my husband and I, who were already struggling to walk in agreement and be on the same page, went through divorce. My daughter and I moved out of our family home and went to live with my parents. We ended up living a couple of minutes from the hospital, we were spending so much time there. Our loving family surrounded us and provided stability and love. I was living moment to moment in total survival mode trying to keep my daughter alive and keep her from regressing and losing more skills and function. She lost her appetite, couldn't sleep, lost language and her ability to learn. If she exercised at the playground more than ten minutes she would have seizures for forty-five minutes and sleep the rest of the day. Our lives were turned upside down. I went back into therapy. I was so exhausted and broken. I felt I lost my child, my marriage, our home, I was completely devastated. I didn't have hope anymore. I was in a constant battle and always on the losing side. That's what I thought anyway.

In 2013 I was able to return to work part time at a non-profit for families with children with special health needs. While working there I learned about a girl like my daughter whose mother had tried giving her Medical Cannabis CBD oil and it had given her a better quality of life. The seizures were reduced and she was growing and learning again. I didn't realize it at the time but I was called by Jesus to move to Colorado. We moved to Colorado Springs so my daughter could begin the CBD oil. As soon as she began taking the medicine her seizures improved dramatically! I had hope again! What I didn't know was that we had just moved into a city of born again, Jesus loving families. We had a new community of families like ours who were trying to help their children heal from Epilepsy. We would go to support groups and the children who were in wheelchairs the month before were now walking in holding the arms of their fathers or mothers. Kids who couldn't speak were talking! Kids who had to be fed through G-tubes were running around eating pizza! I was witnessing real life miracles. I was so thankful we had finally found Hope. Hope for the future! What I didn't know was that it wasn't the cannabis medicine that was healing these children and families. It was Jesus.

After a couple of months living in Colorado Springs I met new friends, women of God who were praying for their children, and began praying for my daughter. They had bible studies and went to church together. One friend gave me the devotional Jesus Calling. I would read it and sometimes I would read it aloud and I could hear the voice of God speaking to me through the scripture and the writing of Sarah Young. I didn't know that He was already transforming my heart. I began listening to worship music and we went to Focus on the Family, had bonfires and barbecues, gathered together for encouragement through our joys and sorrows. The healing was happening. I still was not born again but now I was opening my heart and hearing the voice of God.

Philippians 4: 4-7
"Rejoice in the Lord always; again I will say, rejoice. Let your reasonableness be known to everyone.

The Lord is at hand; do not be anxious about anything, but in everything by prayer and supplication with thanksgiving let your requests be made known to God. And the peace of God, which surpasses all understanding, will guard your hearts and your minds in Christ Jesus."

During one seizure my daughter began talking and telling me that there was an angel who was with her and filling the room with light. She had a beautiful smile and peace and the seizure stopped. After ten months in Colorado we were legally allowed to travel home to Vermont. I was still believing that Cannabis would heal my daughter. It was a long road and her quality of life slowly improved and the seizures eventually lessened.

Returning to Vermont we were reunited with family. I was listening to and singing worship music more and more regularly. I didn't know at the time He was using worship to begin to heal my voice. Our family once again created a nest of security and love around us. And in the place of Peace and Hope for a future we began to live again. My daughter was flourishing working with a local tutor and I got a new job advocating for Special Needs families needing Cannabis medicine. My relationship with the Lord started and I began to talk with Him more and more. I bought my first Bible and began reading the Word of God daily. I began to be stronger and have my own health restored and became physically fit. We were traveling to Maine for a Cannabis medicine that we were not able to get in Vermont. Through the medical Cannabis community I began a friendship with a man of God. I believe the Lord brought us together to be husband

and wife. He has stood by me patiently through these past four years. For four years the enemy brought relentless strife and confusion to the relationship. As a new believer I was so curious and trying to understand my new faith and promises, I was healing from the sin of the past and seeking wisdom to how to walk with Christ. We spent years struggling to find understanding and create balance. Many blessings and many trials came from the time we spent together. Through my faith and the love of the Lord I had my eyes open to see the wounds of my past and to ask forgiveness, receive healing and renew my mind and change the unhealthy patterns. Jesus brought healing to our family but not in how I could have imagined or planned. Sometimes God has a different plan or time and our own minds and hearts do not align with His plan for us. I learned that obedience to God and His conviction on my heart and for my life is above anything that I desire in this precious lifetime He has given to me.

On one trip driving east to Maine I looked up in the clouds and saw Jesus in the sky coming down out of the clouds. I felt pure joy throughout my being. I knew then that I am born again. He filled me with His spirit and Life. I am transforming to be more and more like Him with each passing moment. I am thankful and blessed to be a daughter of the most high King.

There were times in the midst of depression, suicidal thoughts and struggling with wanting or knowing what to live for I have cried out to the Lord to take me to heaven. I remember sometimes when I was so tired and really struggling being a mother and keeping my daughter alive, I asked Jesus, "Lord, take me to heaven now... just for a moment so I can rest." In a breath I was there bathed in warmth and light and love and give faith and hope to continue on this journey with Him.

> ### Isaiah 54:17
> **"No weapon formed against you shall prosper."**

The path is narrow and the enemy can still try to use old memories and wounds to lie and steal the blessings God gives us. I stand in His faithfulness and mercy. I look to Him and trust what He has planned for my life. I am thankful that I have loved deeply, I have a beautiful daughter and family, and loving faithful brothers and sisters in Christ surround us. My daughter is listening and beginning to share her experience with Jesus and the Word of God. We are blessed. I do not know what the future holds but I do know that God wants good for our lives. He wants us to prosper and live a life surrendered to Him. I may be single and a mother but above all I am to be the bride of the love of my life Jesus and for this I am forever humbled and thankful.

During this time God is so good as He brings true brothers and sisters in the Faith to become my dearest friends. I have also witnessed many miracles in our own lives and the people around us. God is so faithful. He is healing our family. By His stripes I believe that she is already healed. Her potential is being restored and activated as time goes on. He restored our health and is redeeming the time for the years that the enemy stole from us. He taught me to forgive myself and that I don't need to be perfect or become something for someone else. I need to follow His voice and when I falter or fail I come to Him seeking forgiveness, comfort and truth. I am learning to be compassionate to myself and gentle. The days that I am struggling I turn my face to Him and I worship with all my heart and pray for godly sorrow to flow from my heart and be transformed for His purpose and glory. God so loves us that each day is overflowing with His tender mercies. My voice is stronger now than ever. I am learning to make good choices for myself and to speak up for what I know is true and who God says I am. I am a daughter of God, the King of Kings and He loves me more than I can ever understand. He has already saved me and I can walk in freedom, strength and love in this life He has given to me.

I am thankful beyond measure that after so many decades of shame, guilt and confusion He was always right beside me walking step by step never letting go and never leaving me and He set me free. Each day He is showing me the way! Thank you Jesus! I love you forever!

Ephesians 5:1-2
"Imitate God, therefore, in everything you do, because you are His dear children. Live a life filled with love, following the example of Christ. He loved us and offered Himself as a sacrifice for us, a pleasing aroma to God."

Shakeela Naz, Pakistani, aged 45, Bishop Majeed Naz Ashiq's wife, born again Christian singer, Gospel singer..

My name is Mrs Shakeela Naz , I am the wife of Bishop Dr. Majeed Naz Ashiq. I was born in a good Christian family on the 30th December 1976. My grandfather was a Sunday school teacher and to this day so many of my grandfather's students are working for the Kingdom of God as Pastors and Bishops. Whenever I meet them they know that I am the granddaughter of Parya Masih. I remember I spent my childhood with him a lot and I learned from my grandfather. When I was in my sixth grade I started to read the Bible by myself .

n my family there was no pastor but when I was a small child I loved to sing. As time went by I had music lessons and later with my Grandfather I started to learn to sing Gospel songs. I studied at a very good Catholic school and I became a member of this Catholic church choir and during my years there I did very well with my studies. They discovered that I had a wonderful voice and I believe God blessed me through my voice because I have won many awards at singing competitions.

I was able to record my winning songs in June 2018 and also three Christmas songs in December 2019 for the Lord and you can watch them on the Youtube channel.

When I was seventeen years old I got baptised and received the Holy Spirit. Then I became involved strongly in a Pentecostal church and I began to pray for the sick and also those people who were affected by the evil spirits so, praise God, He used me in a mighty way in many places in my country of Pakistan.

When I was a single lady I came across many times to Pastor Majeed's meetings and at that time he asked me to do work with him as a Gospel worshipper. While working together I could see in my own eyes that he was a God fearing man so I started praying for a man of God to be part of my life. Finally I told my family about Pastor Majeed and his family, and my family visited their home. We had a good meeting and finally by the grace of God we had a wonderful blessing marriage ceremony on the 10th October 2004.

Because we both are God's servants , our vision is the same to serve Jesus Christ . God blessed us in the first year of marriage, I got pregnant very quickly. When the time came for the delivery I had a natural birth, I was so thankful I had a normal delivery. Now finally we are blessed with five children altogether, but we gave two children to our relatives who are unfortunately not able to have children of their own. In the early days of our marriage we were really struggling financially as my husband was a young Minister in the region of Lahore. I tried to support him whole-heartedly in his studies for his career in the Ministry while coping with our babies at home.

Motherhood is joyful for me but having young children didn't leave me much time on my own hands, but now I am so grateful to the Lord my children are growing up. Isaac is fifteen, Sylvester is thirteen and our daughter Shaina is nine. I can now do more work for the Kingdom of GOD with my husband Bishop Dr Majeed as we work together in unity in the vineyard for the Lord.

I personally felt really blessed when I read KoHsin's testimony 'From HIV to Christ' which was translated by my husband and I learned and thank God how her life was changed by Jesus Christ. Over Christmas 2020 me and my husband distributed so many copies of KoHsin's booklet in the region of Lahore and we have seen how God moves in a mighty way with people coming to know Jesus and miracles and signs follow.

My prayer is that, through working with my husband, we can really see people coming to Jesus Christ and I feel so blessed to have a good marriage and to be the mother of my children.

Claire,
Born again Christian , British.

2 Corinthians 2 :14.
"But thanks be to God who always leads us in triumphal procession in Christ and through us spreads everywhere the fragrance of the knowledge of Him."

I was born in a working class family. My parents worked hard and they married young and they had me and my sisters. I am the middle child. I am very fortunate, I thank God I had a very good upbringing and I was able to travel to a lot of places abroad. But when I was at school I was heavily bullied by my classmates and when I was five years old I was abused by my baby sitter, who was a teenage boy, over a period of six months. One time this young man beat me up so much I ended up in hospital, which is when my parents found out something was seriously wrong with the baby sitter.

When I was a teenager I learned that the man who bullied and abused me ended up in prison and he hung himself in the end which helped me to not feel scared that I will bump into him again. When I turned seventeen years old I was doing a course for hairdressers and living with my friend. One night she woke me up and gave me some drugs to try and I enjoyed it so much, so that was when my addiction to drugs started. I took drugs solidly everyday over a period of two years and I finally had a mental break-down , suffering panic attacks and anxiety and I was taking anti depression pills and got counselling which helped me to take less drugs.

That is when I decided to slow down the drugs I was taking so I just took drugs once a week and took less and less but the addiction was still there. At this point I was already wondering "Does God really exist and can He help me? "I remembered I asked a friend how to pray to God, she said " You need forgiveness!" One day I bumped into a friend of mine who got saved so I asked her where she was going and she replied she was going to Bible study. I found out which church she went to and asked her if I could go with her. I went to church a couple of times on Sunday mornings.

One Sunday morning I felt a strong urge to go to church. When I got there after worship they did an altar call to come up to the front and get prayer. I went up to the front and the Pastor's wife asked if I needed forgiveness for anything. I replied "I've got too many things to ask for forgiveness!" She said "They are all forgiven in Jesus Christ." That day I gave my life to Jesus!

I was instantly set free from all my addictions and physically and emotionally healed! God just start turning my life around. I was dyslexic as I couldn't read properly then suddenly I could read!

I still kept going to church. That is where I met my husband who was an African man who had come to Bradford to study. Then he told me he was very serious about me so we got married. After we got married I tried the contraception pill but it made me so unbalanced and affected my emotions and hormones so I came off the pill. I got pregnant after eight months and I had a very difficult pregnancy because I experienced very bad side effects right through pregnancy including tiredness and pain in my hips which affected my walking. I gained a lot of weight and at times I had cramp pain in both of my legs and my appetite was upside down. It was a hard pregnancy.

The day my baby was born I was induced because the baby was late and when the waters broke they were green. We thought the baby was at risk so my mum said we have to hurry to the hospital. I was in pain for over twenty-one hours and finally the hospital told me I needed to sign the consent form and they rushed me in to have an emergency C section. There was a high risk the baby and I could be harmed as I had a really strong reaction to the epidural. My body went into shutdown mode. The doctors told me my baby inside me was at risk so I remember hearing my husband whispering into my ears with scriptures and encouragement and speaking life over me and the baby, again and again. I came through the operation and the baby was taken away for antibiotics to make sure it had no infection. I suffered a lot of pain after the C section but still decided to breast feed the baby. I fell in love with my baby instantly and I knew it's a blessing from the Lord. I always wanted to have a child and my husband and I were overjoyed and thanking God for our first born.

God helped us to get our first house and we got a very good deal on a house in a nice area. My husband got a new job but his old job paid him in advance and his new job paid him in arrears which left us without any income but miraculously we got a tax rebate that we didn't apply for and it covered the income for that month!

Later on my faith become stronger and stronger as I grew in God. After this I had two more children and I am so thankful to God. Before Christ I was addicted to drugs and my mental health was a mess but now I am completely set free. I know I have a purpose to live for the Lord. I now serve at my church. I also want to tell the readers that what I learned as a mother is that the unconditional love I had for my children is NOTHING compared to how much God loves us! Through the years God has let me become less selfish and all the ugliness inside me is gone and I have learned to cherish my children as they grow. I know if I didn't know Jesus my life would still be miserable and messed up. Now I am so grateful to Jesus who delivered me from the chaotic life I was living and I thank God for the life He has given me.

Elizabeth Mc Allister-McDonald , Age 55,
American, Catholic

I was pregnant when I was twenty-eight years old. Me and my husband had known each other since high school. We were high school sweethearts. I was on the pill for a long time then finally we decided to get married, bought a house and settled down. As soon as I was off the pill, I got pregnant so quickly - only six weeks. My pregnancy journey was very difficult as I needed to go to hospital three times a week because I was at high risk of having a premature baby and in the late stage I was totally hospital-bound. It was not fun. Somehow my baby was very stubborn and my first baby was overdue so the hospital had to induce me, I had all the painkillers you can think of, still the inducing plus long hours of labour exhausted me.

I decided on no breast feeding. I used bottle feed so I am not going to be tied down for a long time with the crying baby. I lost my job during this time and our finance was very difficult. On top of that, nine months later I got pregnant again. I was very angry with my husband at this point as I don't want to have a baby so quickly, however it happened! Again I have a new born to feed plus I am hospital-bound again due to my health issues. In order to save the baby they put me in a room and upside down. I am glad the second child was fine and it was a beautiful girl. After two extremely difficult experiences I decided to tie my tubes and closed my womb. I had the operation done, therefore I will have no chance to get pregnant again.

Motherhood was hard, however because I know both babies are such a blessing to me, and I had such difficult pregnancy and birth, still I love them equally and so much. I found it very hard in the early years because we have no money, my husband was self-employed and I lost my job. Financially we were really struggling. You try your best to provide for them on the little money we have. Also, we found out that my second child she had learning disability after the age of three. At first the school didn't find out and didn't do anything to help. I was furious and I started joining school volunteers and groups to make sure my baby girl will get the help she needs. It was very hard because I had to find out all the resources on my own. I finally know what was the main reason my child was behind and I did all I can to help her to continue to go to school and finish her education. That was very hard on me because I gave all my effort to help my learning disabled child.

When I look back I had two beautiful children and I am glad I have them. Now every Christmas we gather together and give thanks. Motherhood is hard, you never stop worrying about them, still you enjoy the process with them growing up with you together. My baby girl, she is twenty years old and this year I just attended her graduation at college. I am so proud of her I can't describe in my words, however I know I love her always. I continue to pray for my two children everyday even though they are grown into a young man and women.

Psalm 17, 6-8
"I call on you O God for you will answer me, give ears to me and hear my prayer. Show the wonder of your great love, you who save by your right hand those who take refuge in you from their foes. Keep me as the apple of your eye, hide me in the shadow of your wings."

Mary Wu, Age 66, Hong Kongese , Born Again Christian.
President of Aglow International, Republic of China (R.O.C)

Joshua 24:15
"But as for me and my household, we will serve the Lord."

Romans 8:28
"And we know that in all things God works for the good of those who love Him, who have been called according to His purpose."

I married my husband when I was thirty-one years old in Canada. He was a brilliant pastor and we served the Lord together by running a church. We were happily married and within a year I got pregnant. I gave birth to a son. We were both so excited to become parents. I felt so blessed and I really enjoyed being a mother. My birthing experience was extremely painful though, because I insisted on not using epidural as I wanted a natural birth. It felt like a knife was scraping me from the insides repeatedly until the baby was born. At that time I thought there's no way I could go through that kind of pain again. However, when I got pregnant with my second child, I completely forgot about the pain but instead I was overjoyed with having a daughter.

When my daughter was eight months old, my husband contracted a virus and fell very ill. When my husband was in the hospital, we said God's will is higher and when he passed away I knew it was God's will to have my husband return to heaven.

I remember once when my kids were arguing nonstop and I reached my breaking point because I simply just felt like I could not handle it anymore as a single mother. I didn't think and said "I don't love you anymore, stop arguing." Even though I lost my temper, the Holy Spirit immediately reminded me to say "but Jesus loves you". After I calmed down, I realised how deeply regretful I was to have said that I didn't love my children and I promised them to never say those words again.

Because of the unexpected death of my husband, I found it very hard to accept. I knew I needed my parents' support so I moved to Ottawa where they lived. I knew I needed some time to quietly be on my own to process my grief and to clearly think about how I should live my new life and how I could best raise my children so I went to visit my sister in Turkey by myself for two weeks. When I got back to Ottawa, sometimes I would still have the urge to cry at night. I didn't want my children to hear so I would silently cry under my blanket, but I knew I had to lean on God to pull through as I had to be strong for my children. So I focused all my energy on raising my two young children.

One day, my son came back from nursery after seeing all his friend's dads come back from business trips and asked "where is Daddy and when will he return from heaven?" as my son thought heaven was a place on earth. My son would cry out how he wants Dad to hug him and how he misses his father. Seeing my son in tears, my heart would ache and I didn't know how to respond at first, but I prayed and said "Daddy will not be back but you have your heavenly father who will watch over you from heaven". To my surprise, my son stopped crying and said "That means I have two daddies now".

Two years after my husband passed away, it finally dawned on me that I am a single mother without a husband to take care of my children together. The responsibility of raising two children all on my own was overwhelming and so my in laws suggested that I seek counselling. The three of us ended up seeing a psychiatrist. During counselling, I realised even though it may be difficult to raise my children alone, still my children were fine. They have such wonderful memories of their father, and I try my best to give them everything they need.

It was hard to raise my children on my own but I did it with a lot of help and I am so grateful God is always there for me. My children now are both mature Christians and I love them so much. I still travel regularly to see them. I never remarried because now my calling is as an international missionary and I want to serve the Lord Jesus Christ. Amen!

Claire Madrara age 45
British Born again Christian

I was pregnant when I was thirty three years old and I really wanted a family. I am a Christian. I suffered two miscarriages. After the first miscarriage, I don't know why I just continued keeping praying because deep down I really wanted a family with my husband. The first child was dead at thirty-four weeks. It was a very hard day for me - I knew something was going so wrong but I couldn't pinpoint what went wrong and it died and I was heart-broken. We tried again and I got pregnant again but I was so scared things would go wrong and I had a second miscarriage. During this hard time I kept praying and crying out to God and many people were praying for us. I was reading a book called "Super Natural Pregnancy" and this book give me a lot of courage and I tried the third time. Finally I had my first beautiful daughter called Abigail. I had so many check ups with her - first was six weeks, twelve weeks, fifteen weeks, twenty weeks, thirty weeks, thirty-four and finally I had Abigail. NHS were really brilliant with me, they did regular check-ups in order to put my mind at rest and to check everything is ok because I had two miscarriages before and I am so blessed to have Abigail, she is such a happy beautiful daughter.

Then because me and my husband want a big family we kept trying. My second, a healthy boy, is Cyrus who is a special boy to me. The pregnancy was straightforward. Again the NHS kept on top of everything and I had Cyrus and I was in TLC special clinic. NHS gave me the best care I could have had and when Cyrus was born he was fine. Later on at eighteen months old we and the nursery started to figure out he had severe autism. It was the Nursery that identified it first and later on we were referred to see a doctor and specialist regarding his autism. I felt with Cyrus I wanted to give him the best love and attention I can because he is very difficult. It was a daily struggle for me being a mum with an autistic child but still I love him to the end of the world. The school and my husband give me a lot of support but up to today it is still a daily struggle with my boy Cyrus. Also it was so hard that I had sleep deprivation with Cyrus because he was just such a difficult baby. This year the school is helping me to find the best school to provide for his special needs and I am so grateful. I love my son so much but I always need to try to put extra effort towards Cyrus' needs and that makes my motherhood so hard. Still I am not complaining because I know God gave me Cyrus. He is a special son.

My third child is now lying next to me and she is so beautiful and precious because I thought I couldn't get pregnant again. By this time I was forty-four years old and the doctor and my husband both think there is a very tiny chance I will get pregnant again. I was just shocked and scared at the same time when I found out I was pregnant with Georgia. She is a miracle baby. Again I had all the tests and regular check-ups with this baby and she was born in May 2016 and I am so blessed to have her in my life. Now I have three children, which is the big family I always wanted. I prayed for a big family and God has granted my prayer. It is very hard being a mum with three, still I love them equally and I love them so much I wouldn't change them for the world. My first daughter is so caring and lovely, my son Cyrus has special needs but still he is so lovely too and my baby Georgia she is just a blessing in my heart especially. All three of them are in my life and my husband is a good husband, he is very good with them. I am also very blessed as my dad and my sisters pass on so many free clothes so I can have things without spending too much money and when I find it hard to survive with three children I pray to God to give me strength everyday, especially in those early days to overcome my struggle with the two miscarriages. That was a difficult time, but I just didn't give up. I continued because I really wanted to be a mum and my prayers were so strong I knew God would give me a family eventually and now I do thank God.

My biggest struggle with being a mum is sleep deprivation because it was so hard, lack of sleep day in and day out. I knew I wanted a family but with lack of sleep I can't function properly and I know I have to keep on top of things, being a mum of three and I pray every day to do the right thing for my children, Abigail, Cyrus and Georgia. I love them so much and I know in God they have a heavenly father who loves them too.

Psalms 139. v 1-3
O Lord you have searched me and you know me. You know when I sit and when I rise; you perceive my thoughts from afar. You discern my going out and my lying down; you are familiar with all my ways.

v. 13-15
For you created my inmost being; you knit me together in my mother's womb. I praise you because I am fearfully and wonderfully made; your works are wonderful, I know that full well. My frame was not hidden from you when I was made in the secret place, when I was woven together in the depths of the earth. Your eyes saw my unformed body; all the days ordained for me were written in your book before one of them came to be.

Margaret Lee Thomas, age 46, American, Born-Again Christian

I was raised in a loving Christian home with four siblings. My Mom was a stay-at-home-mom and my Dad worked as an Economist at Auburn University. Both parents were educated, and I was very blessed to have a middle-class upbringing and a normal, happy childhood. I am so grateful for my parents and all they have done for me.

I met my husband, David, at church one rainy Sunday evening. I was sixteen years old and he was twenty-four, but despite the age difference, we became friends. Four years after meeting, we began dating, and after we both finished our university degrees, we were married. My husband has always loved children, and we knew we wanted to have a family together one day. We just didn't know when.

We decided to wait to start a family because we both wanted to pursue corporate careers. Three years later we moved to Texas, due to David's new job opportunity, and decided now was the perfect time to start our family. I anticipated becoming pregnant very quickly and even had the timeline of how things would go and how many years apart each child would be, all planned out in my head. It should be easy, I reasoned. My friends and family members could get pregnant quickly, so I didn't think our experience would be different. I never anticipated that we were about to embark on one of the most challenging journeys of our life. By the time we reached the end, every plan, hope, and dream would be shattered into a million pieces.

Shortly after our move, we began trying to get pregnant, and at first, I wasn't worried when it didn't happen quickly. However, after a year passed without success, I became concerned and started discussing options with my doctor. He gave me a low-level fertility drug and within a few months, I became pregnant. We were so excited! It finally looked like our plans were back on track! A couple of weeks later, however, I began bleeding heavily and had a miscarriage. We were devastated and I grieved deeply for many months over the loss of our child.

Amid this grief, we continued pursuing our goal, but I did not get pregnant again. We were now two years into what had become an incredibly emotional, disappointing journey and I was desperate to have a child. At this point, I knew we needed more specialized help, and I asked to be referred to a fertility specialist in Houston, Texas. For the next two years, we endured multiple invasive, but ultimately unsuccessful, fertility treatments. We spent thousands of dollars out of pocket and exhausted almost every option available to us. Nothing we tried worked. Nothing. It began to look hopeless.

As each disappointment came and months passed, I struggled with feelings of anger, resentment, depression, and feelings of failure as a woman. I remember crying out to God many times in prayer saying, "God, I am doing everything *right*. I am in church; I am praying; my husband and I are leaders, and we willingly give our time to mentor young people. We are faithful in our walk with you, and trust you in every aspect of our life. *Why* is this happening? *Why* is it that everyone around me gets pregnant easily but it isn't happening for us? *Why* haven't you miraculously healed whatever the problem is? Where are you? Do you even hear our prayers?" During this time of deep pain and frustration, I had a severe crisis of Faith. I began to doubt that God was listening, and to believe He didn't care about me. I wasn't sure if I could trust God anymore. I felt utterly forsaken and alone. My husband, however, refused to give up. He continued to believe that God had a plan for us no matter what was happening now and we *would* have children.

A couple of years into our fertility journey, David had a dream. In this dream, God showed him a glimpse of our family in the future. We were at an American football game watching one of our children playing on a team. We had three children, two boys and one girl, and they were healthy and beautiful. The dream was so vivid and clear that he woke up feeling very strongly that God would bless us with three children. No matter how hopeless things looked now, children were definitely in our future. I remember him sharing this with me and feeling the first spark of hope after so much disappointment. We clung to this dream and to the prayers of friends and family through the dark days and months that followed.

Finally, four years after seeing different doctors and specialists, they discovered that I had endometriosis. This inflammatory disease didn't present with the usual symptoms so the doctors could not diagnose it without laparoscopic surgery. Through the use of lasers, they were able to remove it all quickly and we began to hope again. A month after my surgery, I finally became pregnant and nine months later, God blessed us with a healthy baby boy named Joshua. We were so excited to have our child! I remember feeling incredibly thankful and relieved to see our hopes and dreams of a family come to fruition. Surely, I thought, our nightmare was over and we had reached the end of this trial!

But, our journey wasn't over. Eight months after Joshua was born, I became pregnant again, this time without any medical help. Things went smoothly in the beginning. We went in for an ultrasound and saw our tiny baby's heartbeat at seven weeks. At ten weeks, we went back for another ultrasound, but they couldn't find a heartbeat. I remember the ultrasound technician looking at me and saying, "I'm so sorry, but there's no heartbeat. Your baby didn't make it." We were devastated. But each time the grief would overwhelm me, I would look at my miracle son and think, "there is hope."

Shortly after that, we moved back to Georgia. Several months later, I became pregnant again. The same thing happened. We went in for our first ultrasound and saw a tiny heartbeat, but they couldn't find a heartbeat at the second ultrasound. This was now my third miscarriage, and I began falling apart, both emotionally and mentally. The grief was more than I could bear some days. The doctors ran multiple tests but couldn't discover precisely why this was happening.

A couple of months after this miscarriage, I unexpectedly became pregnant for the third time. I went to see my doctor (a specialist due to my prior medical history). He decided to try dosing me each day with small amounts of blood thinner during the first trimester as well as extra progesterone and other vitamins. He wasn't sure if this would work, but he said they had seen some success with this particular medical mixture. I was terrified that I would miscarry another baby, and we prayed fervently that it would work.

Nine months later, I gave birth to my second child, a beautiful baby girl, who we named Alana! We were overjoyed to have another child and felt that she would probably be our last child after all we had gone through. But once again, God had other plans. A year after Alana was born, I became pregnant. It was utterly unexpected, so I immediately went back to see the specialist who had helped me with Alana. He gave me the same medical mixture we had used before to prevent miscarriage. Nine months later, I gave birth to my last child, a sweet baby boy who we named Joseph. It was just like David's dream years ago, we had three beautiful children, two boys and a girl! God had truly blessed us with three miracles!

So, after all we had gone through, I should have felt happy and fulfilled, right? But, there was one more unseen battle on my horizon. After my second child, Alana, was born, I couldn't seem to shake the post-natal depression. No matter what I did, I continuously struggled with feelings of inadequacy as a Mom, depression and grief over the three miscarriages, and feelings of failure as a Christian. I was so thankful to have my children, but couldn't stop wondering why it had been such a hard journey for us. Pregnancy and childbirth should be easy, right? Why had God allowed this to happen to us? Why did it feel like He had "singled" us out for a trial that most people wouldn't understand or ever go through? Did we not have enough faith in Him? Why had He not healed us miraculously? Why did we have to use medical help even to get pregnant? Had it been our fault somehow? And the list of questions went on and on. I couldn't seem to shake these thoughts and felt guilty and ungrateful for even feeling these things. I began to draw more and more into myself and struggled to take care of my children every day. It was a constant battle to keep the depression and feelings of inadequacy as a Mom and Christian from overwhelming me.

After one incredibly difficult day, I realized I needed outside help. God enabled me to find a wonderful Christian counselor and she began to help me sort through all the feelings, thoughts, and trauma of the past eight years. In addition, my doctor diagnosed me with Clinical Post-Natal Depression and recommended I take medication to help with the depression. I realized I needed to start taking care of my physical body, so I began to exercise by running regularly. Each day when I would go for a run, it gave me much needed time on my own to clear my head. It also helped me lose the baby weight. I joined a Mothers of Preschoolers (MOPS) group at my church and got to know other moms who were going through the same struggles with motherhood and they helped me see I was not alone. It took a year of counseling, medication and prayer, but I was able to start on the road to recovery and finally get to the place where I needed to be healthy and whole.

During that difficult year of recovery, I realized that as a Christian, I had the wrong expectations of God. His word says He is faithful and has a plan for our life, but His plan doesn't always line up with our plans. His timing is not always our timing; His thoughts are not our thoughts.

Isaiah 55:8.

For My thoughts are not your thoughts, Nor are your ways My ways," says the Lord.

He is God and He is sovereign. He sees what we don't see and understands what we don't understand. Sometimes He will choose to explain why he isn't answering, but sometimes He is silent. I had fallen into the trap as a Christian, where I believed that if I did all the *right* things, prayed all the *right* prayers and said all the *right* scriptures, that God would automatically give me what I had asked for. Basically, I looked at God as a slot machine. If I did all these things, I could pull the handle and out would come my blessing.

Here's the thing, God is not a slot machine, and we can't demand He give us what we want, exactly when we want it. He loves us and wants the best for us and He does hear our prayers, but God is so much bigger than what we know and understand. He sees from the beginning to the end of our lives. He always has a plan, timing and purpose in everything we go through. We may never understand *why* He does or doesn't do something, but through it all we can trust Him and know He is in control. He knows what is best for us. He deserves our honor and worship simply because He is God, and He is holy. If He never did anything else for us, but send Jesus to die, that is the greatest gift we could ever receive, and it is more than we deserve.

Was asking for children and wanting children a bad thing? Absolutely not! Scripture says children are a blessing and a heritage from the Lord (**Psalms 127:3**). He wanted to bless us with children and planned to give us children, but our timing wasn't His timing. Our children came at the right time and during the right season, though we didn't see it at the time.

God also changed my way of thinking and so much more through this trial. I now have a tremendous amount of compassion and empathy for anyone who has gone through the loss of a child or struggled with infertility. I never realized the deep pain a miscarriage can bring and how alone so many feel when they experience this. It's a real loss and there is real grief as you have to surrender those lost hopes and dreams for that tiny life. I realized how each pregnancy is truly a miracle and each tiny life is so very precious. Our medical technology is wonderful but God is ultimately the giver of life. When I hear of friends or family members who are struggling through miscarriage or infertility, it has enabled me to relate to them and comfort them in ways I could not before.

It's been twelve years since my last child was born, and I can look back now and see God's hand working through every painful moment we went through. He never left us, not even in my darkest days of doubt and unbelief. Even when I felt hopeless, forsaken and unloved, He was there and He carried us through. We can trust God. He is faithful and I give Him thanks for everything He has done for us!

Jenny Madden, age 73, born again Christian, British

At the age of fourteen I overheard my Mum talking with the school doctor, she asked if he thought I'd ever be able to have babies. His reply was something like this, if she can find someone that would want to marry her then you would have to take her to the hospital to see a gynaecologist and they would be able to tell her better but in his opinion NO. Well, I had never heard of one of them so found out they were a baby doctor! I didn't understand and thought he was saying that I would never be a mum. I then rebelled as I just wanted to have a baby and I became extremely promiscuous. I had sex with most of the boys who asked me out. I must say that I didn't understand about love and if he told me he loved me I believed them. This was in the 1960's and "Free Love" was in vogue.

Eventually I found myself pregnant at the age of eighteen, thinking the dad would want to marry me, but I was wrong. My Dad was angry and I realised that I had let him down but I only had one focus in life. I went to live with my big brother, his wife and family and they took good care of me. I attended the maternity clinic and had to endure an internal examination each time, they said because I was unmarried. I gave birth to my son in the Maternity Hospital where the matron was very abrupt and didn't like me speaking to other girls, most of whom were giving their babies up for adoption. I went home to my brother's house but it wasn't long before my Mum and

Dad came to visit and asked me to consider returning to them.

My Mum said she would look after my son so I was able to return to my work as an office manager in Liverpool. I hated leaving him with her and felt extremely jealous as she showed him more love than she had ever showed to me. (My Mum was abandoned to a school by her father aged four when her mother died). So when I had the offer from a neighbour to look after her son's children I jumped at the chance.

I moved into his home when my son was eight months old and when he was four years old I married my employer. We had thirty-nine years of marriage before he died and he was a perfect father to my son. Unfortunately we were never able to have a child of our own but we had my son and his two children.

I am very proud of my son. He married and has three children and nine grandchildren. That not only makes me a proud grandma but also a very proud great grandma. I wrote to my son a few years ago to apologise as to how he was brought into this world and he was very understanding and said that I had given him a good childhood and had nothing to be forgiven for.

Through these years I suffered a lot of ill health, as did my hubby but we stuck it out together through thick and thin. When he took ill with throat cancer we both came to faith in our Lord Jesus Christ who has forgiven me for all my past and I am now married to a wonderful Christian man who has taught me the true meaning of love and marriage.

This means I now have: three more stepchildren, six more grandchildren and one more great-grandchild.

Who says that God doesn't answer prayers? I wanted a large family and I've certainly got one now in my seventies.

Nehemiah Chapter 8 Verse 10,
"The Joy of The Lord is my strength".

Terri Burgwin , Born again Christian,
American , Pastor
"I call Him faithful"

I was born and raised in a very spiritual family to which my grandfather was my pastor. I had always been taught the importance of a Christian family and how God views them. I was not a virtuous woman when I married my husband, who then was a minister in one of the local churches. When I married my husband, I had always believed that we would remain faithful to one another and, more importantly faithful to God. During the first few months of our marriage, I noticed a significant change in his behaviour. There were arguments that would stem from out of the blue. Each time these arguments would arise, he would utter another woman's name while he was in prayer. I was totally devastated. This strange behaviour would happen after every argument. After a few months of our marriage, I had my first child. He was my pride and joy. His father loved him, but not enough to stay by our side. He would eventually leave months after my son was born, although it wasn't for a long period of time, it felt like forever. The stress of being a newlywed, having a new baby and the expectations from our church to be a good wife and mother was simply overwhelming.

He eventually came back, and not long after I found myself pregnant again. The thoughts that lingered in my mind were horrifying thoughts of me being a single mother with two sons to raise on my own. I tried everything I knew to keep my home intact, only to find out his truth, which was, his heart was with another woman. This perhaps was more devastating than raising my children alone. His behaviour never changed, he would become so mentally and emotionally abusive that it was as if I was walking on eggshells every single day. I felt as though I needed an outlet to retain my sanity. I then enrolled in nursing school, only to find him becoming even more aggressive and hostile. Yes, there were minimal days where our marriage seemed normal and he showed love, this was when I found myself pregnant again! To say the least, I was horrified. His erratic behaviour would cause bouts of depression, anxiety, and fear. He continued to leave our home for months at a time, and this went on for several years.

During these periods I could only rely on God. I had to totally depend on God to feed us, to clothe us, and to house us. During the times when there was very little food to eat, my prayer was for God to sustain my children; and He did. I prayed and prayed for God to hear my petition and send a miracle. Not long after this prayer, I could hear a quiet voice prompting me to walk to a Catholic church about two minutes from my home, when I got there all I could see were candles lit throughout this beautiful church. Tears rolled down my face as I was the only one there. I prayed one final prayer that God would send a miracle as I prepared to vacate. As soon as my foot hit the last step outside the church, I was approached by a woman going into the church, who asked if she could help me with something. I told her of my dilemma hoping she could be of some assistance. It was at that point, she asked for my address and said she would be in touch. Not more than an hour had passed when my doorbell rang with three angelic women come with bags filled with groceries and additional gifts. As the tears rolled down my face, my soul exclaimed that God is an on-time God! He has always been faithful to me and my children

Psalms 37:25 says,

"I was young and now I'm old, I've never seen the righteous forsaken, nor his seed beg for bread."

God has always been the source of all that was needed in our home, our provider, sustainer and even our protector. Once on my way to work, I left the house and told the sitter to keep a close watch on my children. As I proceeded to drive down the street, something told me to turn around and check on the children. As I approached the street which my house was on, I saw one of the neighbours carrying my oldest son, (who at that time was elven years old,) out of the woods. I immediately drove up to my neighbour frantically, I asked what happened? He replied; "Your son fell out of a tree house!" I jumped from the front seat of the car and placed my son in the backseat of the car and immediately drove to the hospital.

Once we arrived to the E.R. they had him taken him immediately. It was determined that the tree house in the woods was two storeys high. It was only through prayer and the grace of God that my son was able to walk again. During his hospital stay, it was determined he had suffered temporary paralysis. After several weeks in the hospital, one of the doctors stated to me that "someone upstairs is looking down on your son."

In conclusion, as a single mother, I have witnessed the faithfulness of God to both myself and my children. His Word declares that I have never seen the righteous forsaken nor His seed beg for bread. Though there were times of challenge, God has always provided a way for us to overcome each obstacle, giving us the power to overcome them all.

Philippians 4 :13
Until we all reach Unity in the faith and in the knowledge of the son of GOD and become mature, attaining to the whole measure of the fullness of Christ .

Florina Habbin. Romanian.
Born-again Christian

"There is no life without God"

Matthew 4, verse 4.
"Jesus answered "It is written: Man does not live on bread alone, but on every word that comes from the mouth of God"

I was born into a Greek-Orthodox Romanian family, with fear of the wrath of God but I had not much knowledge of knowing God neither having a relationship with Him.

I married after I turned twenty. I was keen to lead and administrate my own life, which soon demonstrated a massive wrong decision, especially after I found out my husband contracted a STD whilst I was over three months pregnant. Abortion was not a solution because we lived under the communist system in 1988 and it was forbidden, so I had to start carrying my cross. Luckily, I gave birth to a beautiful healthy child but I knew my life will not be the same as I dreamt of.

After five years into this marriage, struggling and trying to fight against all the odds, trying to educate my husband. He always apologised, telling me he loves me and our son. We had good communication but when he went out with friends drinking he would have ended up in someone else's bed for a few days, and I realised that I cannot live with fear and anxiety and I don't want to live that kind of marriage.

At age twenty-five, I was a young divorced mother with a child, going back to university to finish my studies and make a new life, but no matter how good and qualified I was I had to live with the stigma of being a divorcee at that young age. Nobody wanted a divorced woman with a child at that young age, in my culture I was not accepted.

I had to live my life being lonely and trying to find someone to be my other half and feeling weak until one day when I decided that I will leave my country for good. I was heartbroken, I saw no future for me there. Thus, I had a wonderful job in a high position in import-export industry. I was respected as a professional woman but I was targeted as a divorcee, vulnerable to men.

After a long battle with myself, the unavoidable fact happened, I left everything behind, my career, my parents, my son and I ran away to the West under the illusion that it would be a better life for me somewhere out there. I was emotionally drained.

I lived in Germany for five years, as long as my visa lasted. I changed my job, learnt new skills, changed my mind set and had a different approach to life. Also, there I met someone and I gave birth to two more children. It wasn't important to me if I would have got married or not, I felt that the whole world was mine.

I was a proud mother of three children, independently living and working, a strong character and emotionally strong, until one day when I received a phone call that my mother had passed and my family had already buried her without me. My father was suffering with a heart condition and the doctors kept him sedated and apparently my sister and the rest of my family couldn't find me, as nobody knew exactly where I lived to tell me about my mother. One day, after much telephoning, one of my nieces finally tracked me down and told me. It was a big shock for me, I had no one close where I could go and cry away my sorrows, my daughter was six months old and I suffered a nervous and emotional breakdown! I couldn't cry so much because of my daughter, I couldn't grieve away my pain.

I had to give up my life in Germany and I returned home to live with my father and look after him. However, back home those years were the most beautiful and memorable years for my children, they got to knew my father, his kindness and his good-cooking skills. But after another five years I found myself alone again, physically and emotionally alone. I lived with the hope that my youngest children's father would come for them but it didn't happen and I was getting older. I was thirty-seven, with three beautiful and intelligent children. I did have a good job in Romania, earning very well but working twelve to sixteen hours every day in a demanding but uncertain industry and it wasn't the life I was dreaming of. My dream was to be a good wife, to have a healthy marriage, one husband only, marriage for my whole life… and yes, I did want a husband again, and I prayed for a husband and I met someone through my job. He visited Romania and we got to meet and know each other for some time before marrying him and following him to the UK. It had been again a tough decision for me to take, it was not all about me now and my needs, I had my three children to think of and my old father too.

I ended up coming to UK in 2006. It had not been an easy transition, especially the first month. It had been quite hard for my youngest children to make friends at school until they spoke the language. It had not been easy and my father had passed away few months after. I couldn't find a job in UK even with so much experience in import-export and references available, although I worked with the international law for freight and moving goods and everything internationally I never passed my interview stages and I decided to change my career.

In 2009, I was already forty-one, I decided to advance my studies in the UK, and went for a degree in health and social care. The thing is, I so much wanted to be housewife material but also wanted to be financially independent especially seeing that my marriage wasn't going well. My husband was addicted to video games, pornography and at least twice a year he would travel to Thailand for one or two weeks to 'have fun in the sun' - cheap and cheerful. Hence, in 2011, we separated and I divorced him due to his unhealthy behaviour.

My life was becoming my kids, my work, my studies, until 2016 when I was invited to attend a church meeting and three weeks after that I asked Jesus Christ into my life as my Lord and Saviour. Amen.

My life has been better since, physically, emotionally and spiritually; there had been lots of challenges and frictions between me and my children because I wasn't the same anymore. I couldn't put up with the nonsense going on in the world but I prayed to God Almighty for my children to come to know Christ and live their lives loving and fearing God. Therefore I have to be grateful and say Thanks to the Almighty that after five years, my prayers have been granted, all my three children are born-again Christians, they love God and I know they will live a good life in Christ.

Now at age of fifty-three, I am surrendered to God and in my heart I have hope that I will live and love again and my story is yet to be written.

Psalm 23, verse 4
" Even though I walk through the valley of the shadow of death, I will fear no evil, for you are with me your rod and your staff they comfort me .

Karen Griffiths. Age 55,
Born again Christian, British.

I have been married twice. My first marriage was when I was twenty-four and it didn't work out so I got divorced two years later. When I was twenty-nine years old I got married again and in six months time I become a new Believer. I was a new baby Christian. My and my husband met at the church and we got married very quickly.

A few months later I got pregnant as a newlywed and I got through the pregnancy well and I gave birth to my first born baby girl. While I was at the hospital my labour only lasted around five hours and up to this day I really thank God she was such a beautiful and healthy baby girl. I started breast feeding with my baby and soon I realised that I'd not really become attached to her. I am a women who loves to have the house clean and tidy and I can't cope with the huge mess. How come a baby can make such a huge mess and turn my world upside down? Because I was on my own most of the time while my husband at work, I used to make a whole list of things I needed to do, and if I couldn't do it all I would feel as if I was a failure. I am not good enough and I'm failing as a mother. Lack of sleep and lack of help was a big thing for me even though I did have a good nurse and health visitor to come and visit me.

After my first baby I quickly got pregnant again. This time my hormones were completely upside down and in few months I lost so much weight so I went to see the doctor. During the doctor's visit, deep down I knew I was depressed and not happy but still I was pretending everything is OK. After the doctor's visit I started taking anti depression pills and by this time I had a toddler to look after and also I had another baby who needs me. I was tired all the time and I realised that the anti-depression pill just numbed the pain I had inside of me. Because I am a Christian and a church goer I remembered one time when I reached out to someone at church, that the lady just said " I will pray for you" and she started quoting scriptures at me but then I realised it's not helpful at all so I stopped and I just kept all the feelings and pain to myself and retreated into my shell.

I am a person who, on the surface I can really pretend everything is fine but then I can lose it in a second! I remember I even helped with running a church toddler group and feeling "I can do this on top of everything" but still I was dying inside knowing I have post-natal depression and taking anti-depression pills. Yet I never confided in anyone. I knew I didn't want anyone to judge me or feel I was a failure so I just kept going.

I had fear inside and frightening thoughts and was sad at times or I could be lost in a second, just crying. Because me and my husband want to have three children I followed this idea and got pregnant again. I did have three children quickly all together. Now when I am looking back at my life during those first three to four years I know I was a good mother but it really felt like a blur as this was the darkest time for me in my life.

I remember one rainy day I had an incident while all the children were kicking off and I hit my boy on his head in the pushchair. As soon as I did that I felt so guilty and I managed to walk to the doctor's surgery and asked to speak to my Health Visitor. I had a complete mental breakdown. I had all sorts of feelings of guilt and felt useless and worthless and my doctor did hear me out and I am back on medication straight away!

Thankfully later on my father- in-law moved in with us so I started having a bit of free time and I had someone willing to help with childcare. Also by then we decided to move to Shipley and we joined the Christian Life church. I believe God helped us to move there and I started having some really good friends that became my support system. I start to feel more myself and when I look back I believe God didn't give up on me as I said I was a new believer.

I also want to share when I was really down or when my baby was having a nap I used to turn on the TV and watch the GOD channel. I used to find so much comfort in watching them especially the women's ministry and when they shared their struggles on the screen I found comfort and I prayed and knew I was not really alone. I also believe the women's ministry has helped me so much during my dark time. You see those years were hard because I was on my own with three kids, and while I am pretty good at pretending everything is good on the outside, I knew I was dying inside and as for the pain and the depression feelings I had, I just buried them into a box and pretended they were non-existent. Finally, slowly, after we made a move to another church God started to bring good friends around me. Slowly and gradually I received a lot of healing from God; one of the healings was so significant including breaking the generation curse so my whole family were saved.

Now I truly want to thank God because I knew He is faithful and, yes, He never gave up on my family and I have overcome through the years and received healing. Even when I was faithless in the beginning God still had His hands on me and was helping me to come out those darkest times so I know I will be forever thanking HIM and Praise HIM.

Isaiah 44 :6
"This is what the Lord says, Israel's King and Redeemer , the Lord Almighty I am the first and I am the last. Apart from me there is no God ."

Acts 1: 8
"But you will receive power when the Holy Sprit comes on you and you will be my witness in Jerusalem

and in all Judea and Samaria and to the end of the earth
."

I am grateful to KoHsin for inviting me to share
my faith testimony of the blessings and challenges of
motherhood. I hope to express both in ways that
demonstrate how God's hand has been reaching to
redirect me when needed, guide me along this circuitous
journey, and work in astonishing ways.

My husband and I met in an uncommon way. He
was in a band seeking a bass guitarist and singer, and I
was a singer and bassist looking for a band after my
previous band had broken up. A week after I moved to
Pittsburgh, I walked into a music shop and found a
musicians' magazine where my husband's band placed an
ad. That evening I called the number and we talked about
his band, music styles and goals. I had hopes of getting on
the road and playing professionally. I remember as he
talked about his desires to settle down with a family
someday, wondering, "Why is he thinking about 'settling
down' at this point of life?" It was something that didn't
cross my mind in my early twenties as music was my
primary focus. We nonetheless began playing music
together, and this was the beginning of our friendship.

I would describe my relationship with God at that
time as knowing He was there, but I was not actively
following Him. I wanted a new life away from my
hometown and, along with difficulties I wanted to leave
behind, I wasn't leaving God much room to work in the
life I thought I wanted to create for myself.

As a kid, I loved learning about God and sensed
His closeness through nature. My family went to church
every Sunday. I would sing hymns as I hiked the
mountain behind our house and would sing in church.

But in response to dysfunction while I was growing up, a poor relationship with my dad, and things introduced to me that were inappropriate for a young child, I developed an inconsistent relationship with God, unhealthy go-to's, and eventually unhealthy relationships throughout my teen years into my twenties.

During my eighth grade year, I suffered severe depression and I was hospitalized for six weeks. When I returned to school, I was mocked and labelled "crazy," and worse. And the problems at home increased. Though our family went to church, and I experienced God's closeness through music and nature, I didn't know how to apply God's love and His word to my pain. The things that were introduced to me when I was too young to process them had more influence on me than my church experience did. I welcomed attraction from boys as a form of acceptance that contrasted those who bullied me for being 'sent away' for the depression. As I sought relief from both rejection and problems at home through relationships, I developed the inability to commit to any of them.

When I graduated high school, I wanted to get away from my home town and I determined I didn't want anyone to know about my depression and the labels that followed me from eighth grade until my senior year. I studied music education at a Christian Liberal Arts School in Rochester NY, but later joined a band that played in bars. I moved to Pittsburgh after it broke up and continued on my path to create a different life for myself, and to find another band. This is the point where my husband and I met through the musicians wanted ad, eventually began dating and making plans for the future. But my inability to commit would strike again and, just before we were about to get engaged, I was unfaithful with a roommate in a college co-ed rental house. The jeopardizing of my relationship with my soon to be fiancé, was my ultimate wake up call, and was a time of intense grief and remorse. I looked at myself in the mirror with loathing, calling the 'so called Christian' looking back at me a hypocrite. "Why can't I live out this life the way I know I should??" For nine months, what faith I had prevented me from taking my own life. I ate very little, laid awake late each night crying, and would pray not to wake up or that an accident while driving to work would take my life.

During that time period, I was leading worship at a Lutheran church. The Pastor was concerned about me as it became evident that I wasn't eating or sleeping well. I told him what happened and that I realized my inability to be a faithful Christian disqualified me from leading worship. His response to this became a turning point in the midst of one of the darkest times of my life. "Why does a pencil have an eraser?" He asked me. "Because we make mistakes," I replied. "Exactly. When we make mistakes, God has provision. Sometimes the tuition is high, but the learning is invaluable." So he urged me to learn everything I could from this costly relationship failure and not give up on myself and to seek God to show me how He wanted to use it.

I sought counselling, took some classes at a community college, learned to cook, got into the Word and journaled. God began to show me the roots that stemmed back to my earliest childhood event which was tied to the tendencies that would ultimately lead to my unfaithfulness to my fiancé. I would still reach out to Him as I sought transformation. I was learning about my fears of commitment and how I looked to others to bring me happiness instead of letting God be my source of healthy love to receive and give. My ex-fiancé would agree to my invitations to dinners I was learning to make, but I was the only one who did the calling. My hopes would plummet when I wouldn't hear back from him. It was increasingly evident the trust was gone and that there was likely no chance of getting back together. But nine months after we broke up, just before my birthday, I found in my mailbox an envelope with familiar handwriting, simply addressed, "Lisa." As I read his letter I wept as mercy and undeserved kindness flooded me. He wanted to spend time with me for my birthday. I was overcome with the joy of another chance and new beginnings. We began dating again, and two years later, we married.

Deep gratitude for God bringing us back together fuelled a desire for a closer walk with Him, and we began attending church. But my job began to require long hours and I was finding myself unable to "turn off" work in the evenings. My inability to find much time or focus for reading the Word or to devote to music added unfulfilled longings to the stress. So having children wasn't on my radar. I thought we would try when we were ready, and when things settled down at work or I found another job. Of course I did not know when that would be. To our surprise, I became pregnant three months after we married. I called my mom, barely able to get the words out, though she knew right away. She asked me what my husband's response was. "Oh yes! I need to tell him!" I cried. We still laugh about this. I was beside myself with joy and excitement. My husband and I were raised in families where our moms stayed home with the children, and agreed upon this for our new family. So the news of my pregnancy was a welcomed solution for my work situation. I would quit as soon as the baby was born.

What I didn't anticipate was the impact that a physical condition, which I have not mentioned until now, would have on my pregnancy. I had reflux since I was kid and had two surgeries as a young adult in attempt to resolve it. As the baby grew, I developed a band of severe, sharp, burning pain in my upper abdomen that made any physical activity, including standing, very difficult. My physician who had performed the second of the two surgeries, had no suggestions for my relief. Any tests required to explore the cause of the pain would be too invasive and potentially harmful for the baby and most pain medicines are not recommended for pregnant mothers. I feared the pain would only increase as the baby continued to grow. I cried out to God, "Father, please help me, I don't know how I will continue to cope with this pain," and, "How will I be able to deliver this baby?"

Around the sixth month of my pregnancy my mom came to visit and to take me to department stores to register gifts for my baby shower. I really didn't know how we would accomplish this as I could only stand for a few minutes before the sharp pain would set in. I was hopeful we would find a wheelchair or something to help me get around the store to select the baby items. On the night before my mom and I were going to register the baby gifts, I arranged my pillows as I would on the couch where I would sleep for elevation and support to ease the pressure of my pain site. In the middle of the night, I was startled awake by the presence of what looked like a man standing at the side of my couch. I couldn't make out his features in the dark, but it seemed he had wavy, shoulder length hair. As I was waking up I found myself exclaiming, "Who are you and why are you here?" As I was saying this he placed his hand on my upper middle, right where I had been experiencing the pain, and then he was gone. I was puzzled about what just had happened and looked around for a while before falling back to sleep.

The next day, I registered for the baby shower with my mom, amazed and overjoyed that I was pain free as I walked around the department stores. I knew I had experienced a miracle through a divine visitation! I had no more problems for the remainder of my pregnancy!

I worked until the day before our first daughter was born. Soon after she was born, I began to attend Bible Studies at a nearby church. A love for God and His word was ignited in my life. I joined the worship team and began to use my music abilities for worship. Becoming a mom who had been given another chance, participating in the miracle of bringing precious human life into the world, and the gratitude I had toward my Healer who freed me from the terrible pain I had during my pregnancy, gave me much reason to devote my life to the One who continued to pursue me and intervene all throughout my wandering years. Two years after our daughter was born, we had our son. This pregnancy went smoothly, although the delivery was too fast to receive an epidural. I was fear-gripped to face the pain of labour and delivery without any pain maintenance. But I discovered that I recovered faster than I did with my first delivery. I was led to choose all natural for my future pregnancy.

As a new mom, I was so grateful God blessed us with our little girl and baby son. I loved being a mom. But the around-the-clock and unpredictable nature of the work of motherhood requires major adjusting! Although I was happier as a mom than at my high demanding job, I didn't have a sense of how well I was doing with tasks that became undone quicker than re-done. My husband began working long hours, and I would look at my to do list at the end of the day puzzled why so many things on the list remained. I would try to make dinner but it was often the time the babies would be their fussiest. I remember sitting on the bed one late afternoon holding both of them, feeling defeated by how little I felt I'd accomplished and no clue what to do for dinner. I held them on my lap while the three of us cried.

But what began to happen as I continued to study God's Word in spite of the busyness, was He would create melodies to the scriptures I wanted to commit to memory. If I had scriptures posted in my kitchen, He would set them to music while I did housework. He was leading me to write songs to help me remember His Word. I shared some of the songs in church, and asked God to show me His plans for the song-writing. One day I felt Him calling me to "record and build a website." So I recorded my first song by the end of that year. He continuously placed new songs on my heart, but it was hard to etch out time to work on the songs with the demands of two small children. At one point I went to the studio to record with the amount of preparation time I could find, but after an hour the engineer said, "Lisa, you just don't have it today."

Lack of confidence, and perfectionism, began to creep in and I also entered a season in which I was no longer invited to share my songs at churches in our area, and I began to become confused about God's purpose for the song writing. Delay also contributed to the discouragement. I was hopeful about finding more time to devote to the music when my son would enter kindergarten. But then baby three, in answer to big sister's fervent prayers for a little sister, was on the way.

After preschool our five year old son said, out of the blue:

"Mom there's a baby in your tummy."

"Oh really? How do you know?"

"God told me," he casually replied. "Is there?" he asked.

"Well, we'll have to wait and find out."

Two weeks later, it was confirmed. He and God were right, and knew before I did! And while I was pregnant with our third baby, my son dreamed I had twins. If he was right about the pregnancy, then he could be right about this too! But the ultrasound revealed one baby. Our third baby, a girl, our oldest daughter's answer to prayer, came two months after my son started school.

The day we welcomed our youngest girl, my dad announced that my step-sister had her baby. I was taken back by how similar the girls' names were, without discussing names ahead of time. After our baby girl turned two, we grieved a pregnancy loss, followed by another. What I learned is that it is true grief to be acknowledged because of the value the little life holds. The days a baby has on this earth do not determine the value of the child. We all grieved. And again, my son had called the pregnancy of the first baby we lost. He said he wanted to name the baby "Jacob."

I am pressing pause now, as I am crying as I write about our losses even though five years have passed. When my third baby girl and step sister's girl were six, we tragically lost my step-sister after she was struck by a car while she was walking to a friend's house. It has been two years since the loss of my step-sister. There is much more I could say as we grieve our loss of my step-sister and consequently bringing our step-niece into our family. But I need to respect the requested length of my story. Her little girl and our third girl would become "sister cousin twins" as they lovingly refer to themselves. She has been with our family for a year now. But this is another remarkable thing God has done, a story line only He could write. I think back to our son's dream about twins. As we have been adapting to bringing a child of traumatic loss into our family, even though we don't understand why things happen as they do, I believe his dream was a sign that God had provision for my little step-niece. She and our youngest are six hours apart in age. God gave our son foreknowledge that we would in fact have twins — non-biological twins — in our family.

When our oldest two were small I recall my husband and I agreeing 'we're not the big family type'; we're content and had our hands full with two children. But God multiplied what we thought we could handle to four children!

In closing, I now bring my story to present day, to this evening. Kitchen clean up and bedtime routine took longer tonight and after a non-stop day of cleaning, grocery shopping, cooking and running kids to their activities, I lean into God in honest conversation. "Lord, I don't know how to succeed at this life You've given me and I don't like this non-stop pace. Sometimes I feel like a

Mary forced to be a Martha, and I want to slip away longer to sit at Your feet."

I find that my husband is snoring so I slip out of the room and step on a dog bone as I head to a couch, spilling my water on myself. Yes, you won't find perfection in this household. But I desire love to be at the centre and that we learn to trust in the One who is perfect. He says He is pleased with us, not because of how we perform, but based on what He has done on our behalf, because of His deep, unconditional affection for us. I am blessed and He provides in so many ways. But I, at age forty-five, still have not figured out how to keep up in a way that I feel satisfied, and it is a continuing challenge to know how to devote the amount of time I desire to music ministry.

But this evening I read the story to my eight year old girls of the five loaves and two fishes that Jesus multiplied to feed the multitude. My music ministry efforts seem like that meagre meal in comparison to the amounts of laundry and dishes produced by a family of six. I am challenged to trust God will multiply and make effective the little time I do devote to the song-writing. I am at a place where I am asking Him to unearth and breathe life onto buried dreams, and lead me in His plan for songs recorded but not shared. He puts the desires on our hearts, so we must cling to His promise to fulfil the plans for the other ways He has designed us to serve Him in addition to caring for our families. Our children are our primary ministry, but we can't dismiss what He has additionally entrusted us to do. My prayer for us moms is that we look to Him for perspective and adjusting expectations, and discern what we can let go of to prioritize what matters most.

I want to encourage you, dear reader, not to let buried dreams and abilities to cause you to devalue or dismiss them. Sometimes twenty minutes is all you may have, but please be true to how He designed you. Set aside what time you can, and make it a goal to do it regularly. We moms must encourage one another to value ourselves by loving well those God has placed in our care as well as loving ourselves by developing the gifts and abilities He has given us. Developing and using them is a tremendous example to our children to develop and use theirs! Do not despise the days of small beginnings. A little in the hands of our God of multiplication can become more than what you or I can imagine. May we moms stay the course and not grow weary in well doing. He makes everything beautiful in its time and there are miracles and treasures along the way. He gives more than enough Grace for the journey. Bless you and thank you for reading my story of God's faithfulness, grace and miracles in motherhood!

Eph 3:2
"Now to him who is able to do immeasurably more than all we ask or imagine, according to his power that is at work within us, to him be glory in the church and in Christ Jesus throughout all generations for ever and ever.

Ecc 3:11
"He has made everything beautiful in its time. He has also set eternity in the hearts of men; yet they cannot fathom what God has done from beginnning to end."

Pamela Healy Nogueira, age 51, Born Again Christian, American, Weight Loss Coach. "Pamela Perfect"

I was blessed to live in a loving, traditional household with a mother who stayed home, a father who worked, and two older sisters who kept me on my toes. My parents moved from Jersey City, New Jersey to the safer, quieter suburban community of Carteret when I was just a year old. We had food on the table, a roof over our heads, a Catholic school and church we were active in, and friends. L ife, for this girl growing up in the 1970s and 1980s, was perfect! And so began my lifelong obsession with perfection.

As a child, I was blessed to do very well in school, usually achieving all A's in my classes. I was the captain of the cheerleading squad. I got the lead role in my high school play. I was confident and happy whenever I achieved my own idea of perfection.

Life was not always my idea of perfect. When I was ten years old, I tried out for a role in our school's play. There were many parts available. I did not get a role, but my sister who was shy, did. That was a failure to me, and probably what motivated me to capture the lead role in my high school play. I took my failure, put pressure on myself to be perfect, and won the role (even learning a Norwegian accent to audition with)!

As a child, I always had high self-esteem. That comes from my parents always encouraging me and helping me to be the best (*not* the most perfect) I could be. My mother always used to say, "As long as you try your best, we will always be proud of you." Notice she didn't say as long as I did everything *perfectly*.

One day, as a developing pre-teen girl, I was outside my home in a bathing suit. A neighbourhood boy

111

came up to me and said, "You're going to be hot when you get older." He also suggested weight loss will help me get there. My dear Grandmother, at the same pre-teen time, began making little innocent comments when I would see her. "Pammy, you look good. Did you lose weight?" My undeveloped brain took both of those comments and registered them as ideals for perfection. When I lose weight, then I will be perfect.

I truly believe the words you hear are the words you endear. I was given the nickname "Pamela Perfect" by my sister's friend when I was in the 6th grade. I don't know what I did to earn that distinction, but she must have seen my perfectionist tendencies. Thinking back to that year, I can see I was a bit of a know-it-all and a critic of anyone not following the rules I thought were important. If others did not comply, they were less than perfect.

As I got older, I can clearly see pivotal moments in my life when I felt like a total failure because I did not measure up to my idea of perfection: missing Summa Cum Laude honours in college by hundredths of a point; ending the marriage with my high school sweetheart; being laid off in a large company move; collecting unemployment for almost six months and receiving rejection letter after rejection letter; not having a boyfriend when it felt like all of my friends did; etc.

2 Corinthians 12:9
And He said to me, "My grace is sufficient for you, for My strength is made perfect in weakness." Therefore most gladly I will rather boast in my infirmities, that the power of Christ may rest upon me.

In all my trials, I prayed to God to help me fix my situations. I never once gave them over to Him to fix. I thought it was all on me. When I couldn't, I didn't pray more or go deep in the Word; in fact, I never opened the Bible. I reached, instead, for food.

When life felt perfect, I lost weight. When it didn't, I gained weight. It wasn't just extra fat I was carrying; it was the burden of perfectionism I carried with me twenty-four seven. I carried it into motherhood.

On a cold December night in the year 2000, I became a new mom to a bouncing baby boy. It was an easy pregnancy, but my blood sugar level was higher than it should have been. I was put on a diabetic diet, I monitored my blood sugar level several times a day, and I gained the perfect amount of pregnancy weight. He was a big baby, but he was healthy.

In the hospital, I struggled to get him to latch on to my breast for nursing. When I took him home, I really began to panic and fear he was not getting enough breast milk. A woman from a local breastfeeding support group offered to come help me, but I refused. I felt I should do it myself. I failed. I couldn't do it perfectly, so I had my husband buy a can of baby formula. When my son started drinking the first bottle, I felt relieved--partially. I was left with guilt that I could not do what I set out to do.

When my beautiful daughter was born twenty-one months later, I was determined to perfectly nurse her. I had learned that my breasts were too full for a baby to properly latch. Another mother suggested I express a little milk before putting her to the breast. It worked! My guilt was gone. I redeemed myself from my failed attempts at breastfeeding my son.

As my children grew, I tried so hard to be what I considered the perfect mother. I wanted to be my mother! She was perfect in my eyes. I left my exciting career as an international jet-setting software trainer and stayed home to take care of my babies. I cooked meals, I read to my kids constantly, we did a lot of fun things together. Life was perfect... until they went to school.

My son spent first grade getting bullied by some troubled children. It got so bad that with only four months left in the school year, I pulled him out to home-school. I had only recently heard about home-schooling, but I saw it as a way to control the school environment and make it as perfect as I could.

The next school year, I let both of my children go back to school. As soon as I caught wind of something at school that wasn't ideal, I pulled them out to home-school. We had done this back and forth between school and home-school throughout their formative years. I kept trying to make everything live up to my warped ideals of perfectionism.

Around the same time I pulled my son out to home-school, I had given my life to Christ. After I moved from New Jersey where almost everyone is Catholic, to the North Carolina "Bible Belt" where most people are raised Baptist, I was exposed to something new...the Word! God put strong Christian friends in my life; I began listening to Christian radio programs daily; I watched Christian pastors on TBN. Every time I heard Joel Osteen lead viewers in the prayer of salvation, I said it in my mind. Then, one day in June of 2007, I made a confession of my sins, in my bedroom, and asked Jesus to be my Lord and Saviour. I was a new creation! How perfect!

It was not the perfect salvation story to me. After I was saved, I went to both the Catholic church and a non-denominational Christian church at the same time! You would think I would stop going to the Catholic church, but I was the only person in my birth family who was born-again. I knew my parents would be disappointed. I felt like I had failed because I was doing something contrary to my religious upbringing. Such inner conflict plagued me for years! I eventually stopped attending Mass and got involved with a Ladies' Bible Study group. There I learned about having a personal relationship with Jesus. They reassured me week after week that I was saved by Jesus' blood. Thirty-seven years of Catholic theology had made me doubt I would go to heaven when I died. I was taught about purgatory and being prayed out of it when I die. Rules-based religion is easy for a perfectionist to accept; developing a personal relationship with Jesus the Saviour was more difficult.

Through the years, I continued to recite the Prayer of Salvation whenever I heard it at the end of a church service or Christian TV program. I felt like I needed to say it over and over to make it stick! On May 1, 2018, international evangelist Nic Vujicic preached to an area church. My family attended. At the end, Nic had an altar call. Even though I accepted Jesus over and over, I felt a burning sensation in my chest. I knew I couldn't walk out of there if I didn't go to the altar. My husband followed. There, for the first time, I made my salvation public. I guess that's what I needed. I had been "hiding" it while trying to live like a perfect Christian. It was full surrender to God. Tears, sobbing, peace, and relief came to me. Ten months later, I was baptized. I guess I was waiting for the "perfect" moment at my church.

Since then, I have learned to let go and let God. My perfection problem had been revealed to me by the Holy Spirit. I realized I could never make everything perfect, but Jesus did! I am getting better at "giving it to God". He is in control. I am not.

Psalms 18:32
"It is God who arms me with strength, And makes my way perfect.

I am not a perfect mother. I am not a perfect wife - nor a perfect daughter, sister, or friend. I am made in the image and likeness of God. I am a new creation and can stop carrying the unbearable weight of perfectionism on my back. In fact, I have lost one hundred one pounds asking the Lord to work on my perfection problem!

My children are young adults now. May they realize I tried my best to be a good mother and give them as close to a perfect childhood as I could. I want them to see their mother as she truly is - perfectly *imperfect*. I pray they realize it was only through my surrender to God that I was freed from the burdens of weight, guilt, and perfectionism - and He can set them free of their burdens, too!

Marcia Linton. Age 56. Born Again Christian. British. Pastor Spirit of Living Water Church

John 4 verses 13-14.
Jesus answered. "Everyone who drinks this water will be thirsty again but whoever drinks the water I give him will never thirst, indeed the water I give him will become in him a spring of water welling up to eternal life."

I grew up in the middle class area in Leeds. My mum was a nurse and my dad was an engineer. I went to Sunday school and I attended dance classes from when I was a young child all the way up to adult age. As a result, I did so well with dance that I was honoured to be selected for the Olympic Team when I was a teenager. I also learned all different dance moves from different cultures. When I was a teenager I fell in love and got pregnant at a young age. I knew very little about sex education. My mum and dad were very disappointed that I fell pregnant at sixteen, but they supported me throughout my pregnancy. I myself felt ashamed for being a young mother but fell into the role of motherhood very quickly. I am now very grateful for my parents' support and guidance.

During my pregnancy I suffered from very high blood pressure and ended up staying in hospital for three months before I had my first son. Because of my health condition I had to have forceps and an epidural through the birth, because I couldn't have a normal birth. As I had high blood pressure, having a normal birth would cause the death of myself and my son. After my child was born, my parents were so happy and fell in love with their grandson straight away. Because I was so ill, my mum was the first person to hold my son and she still remembers this memory to this day. When my son was six my parents left England and moved to Jamaica. I then had to learn how to bring up my child on my own, learn to take the full responsibility of motherhood and look after my own home.

By the age of twenty-five I was married and had four children, I was living a happy married life and never wanted for anything for my children or myself. My then-husband always provided for us. As the years went on, sadly my husband got addicted to crack cocaine and he became very abusive and paranoid and would sell things from the house for his drug habit. He became violent and he committed adultery so my marriage finally broke down. As a young child I was brought up in a Christian home but never followed the Christian path as a young adult. I decided to move away from the Christian faith and followed the Muslim faith because I had no loving Christian friend around me to keep me on the path of Christianity. Some of my friends decided to turn from Christian to Muslim and I followed. By this time I was now divorced and decided to go to London, my purpose in going was to find peace of mind for two weeks.

I remembered very clearly I packed the Quran in my luggage but, it was supernatural intervention. That day when I arrived in London and I opened my luggage the Quran was not there anymore! I was thinking "When I'm on my period I cannot pray to God." I heard this voice clearly say "You can pray to Jesus when you're on your period". Then I was saying to myself, "How am I going to wash myself on this coach journey before I pray?" Then I heard the same voice again from Jesus "You don't need to wash yourself before you come to me in prayer."

I went to Leeds a month later and visited a Christian friend who I knew from when I was a child. Because I love music and dancing God used this to draw me into Christianity. My childhood friend whom I visited give me a gospel cassette to listen to.

I fell in love with gospel music. I danced in my room, playing it again and again. I didn't know I was worshipping Jesus, still I loved singing and dancing in my own room. That's when I started praying to God more! I did question the Muslim faith because it seems there are so many rules I have to follow to earn favour from Mohamad. One day I walked to the pharmacy and I passed the church on the way. I looked up the service times and that night I was thinking about going to church. I said to the Lord, God I believe in you, you know, but I need to know if you are real. I tried to find you, please show me who you are."

I had had a bad experience at a church in Leeds which made me sceptical of going to any church. Afterwards, I found a church in London and I went to visit this church that I remembered. I walked to this church one Sunday with the live music and singing going on. This church was so alive and I was drawn into it. That is where I met a lovely lady called Judith and people welcomed me with open arms. As time went on I became good friends with Judith and we became prayer partners. She encouraged me with my Christian walk. She took me to a Christian shop and I was overwhelmed by so many things inside the shop. That is when I really had hunger for the Lord. Jesus knew how to hook me through gospel music as I loved to dance and worship all day. After settling into this church I finally got baptised in 1999.

During the years of being a Christian, God really helped me with being a single mum and brought me Christian friends. Later on I had such a vivid dream - I dreamt that I was ordained to become a Pastor. I had to learn so many things through the strength of the Lord and I also learned about deliverance and I did deliverance. In 2012 I was ordained as a Minister, thank you Lord. A few years later God told me to move back to Leeds. I came back to Leeds and that's when a Bishop called me and he said he would like to ordain me to become a Pastor. I officially become a pastor in 2017.

I saw a golden bridge in the sky when I was meditating on the word of God. God was at the one end of the bridge shining brightly and I was holding hands with people of different nationalities, taking them across the bridge to Jesus. There was a sign above the bridge that said "Spirit of Living Water Church" that became the name of my church in 2018. The Lord told me - he showed me a golden bridge and I saw the light coming out from this bridge and there were people walking on this bridge, walking towards to the light. Then the Lord said to start a church called "Spirit of Living Water Church". I had this vision in 2003 and now I am officially running this church for Jesus. Today my passion is to speak the word of God and to spread the gospel.

Today I have four grown up children and five grand-daughters and my children are so precious and beautiful to me. I am so thankful to the Lord that I found Jesus and I know today I am so blessed being a Pastor at Spirit of Living Water Church and I am so grateful that I am able to live out my calling today.

Genesis 50 20-21
"You intended to harm me but God intended it for good to accomplish what is now being done, the saving of many lives. So then, don't be afraid I will provide for you and your children 'and he reassured them and spoke kindly to them."

Luke 10 verse 19-20
"I have given you authority to trample on snakes and scorpions and to overcome all the power of the enemy, nothing will harm you. However do not rejoice that the spirits submit to you but rejoice that your names are written in heaven ."

"THE PROCESS OF BECOMING A MOM"
By Shell Richardson, presenter of "She Speaks" US talk show.
African-American, Christian.

Becoming a mom, for some, may have been one of the greatest experiences one could ever imagine. Looking back over my life and reminiscing over the day of the birth of my first child, I remember that day was full of joy and also great concern. Being pregnant as a teenager was a great challenge. There were days when I thought there was no way I will be able to raise this child. Growing up in a house whereas believing and trusting in God was always taught, I knew that I had to revert back to everything that I had learned. Watching my mom get up and go to work every single day, just to keep a roof over our head, I learned that I really needed to trust God If I was going to make it as a mom.

Being so young and inexperienced, I really struggled trying to make it all work. Having a child at such a young age, I really didn't get the chance to experience some of the things that a normal teenager experienced. I didn't get to go to the school dances, or other outings, which sometimes left me empty and alone. Even though it was hard, I tried my very best to be the best mom possible for my child. There were days when I felt like giving up and throwing in the towel. I dealt with depression, low self-esteem and unworthiness. I would often feel as if I was a failure. I often found myself crying and calling out to God just to get through the day. I knew that no matter how hard things were going to get, that I still had to hold on to my faith in God, that He would see me through.

Somewhere in the back of my mind, I always knew that one day it would all fall in place. Years would go by without ever showing a sign that I would ever become stable enough to accomplish anything on my own. There were days that I would stare into my child's eyes, just to remind myself to not give up because I had to be strong for the both of us.

Finally I was able to leave my parents' house and get my own place. I was so excited! But, I had no idea that things were about to really get rough. Here it is, a young teen with her first place. I was living in the projects, and to some that was shameful. But, to me it was a blessing to have a roof over my head. As time passed, I would later learn that I wasn't just living in the projects. The projects were my processing chamber. Living in the projects was the beginning of God preparing my heart to love Him and to love myself. There were many lessons that I would learn while living there. One of the biggest lessons was to learn how to trust God to keep food on the table, clothes on my child's back, along with clothes on my back as well. Times were very hard for me there, but I gained so many survival skills, the right way. I learned how to survive the right way! I didn't have to prostitute myself or do anything immoral to make ends meet. I just trusted God to provide for me. Waiting on God didn't mean that I wasn't trying to do all I could to better myself as a young mother. I struggled, because I lacked the educational tools to better prepare myself for a world that was moving at such a fast pace. I really desired to go back to school, but trying to raise a child and go back to school was really impossible. Even though I couldn't pursue my dream to go back to school, at that time, I knew that one day I would be able to do so.

I would continue to raise my child alone until years later, I would meet my husband. One day while sitting on the porch at home (mind you, I'm in the projects,) he strolls through my neighbourhood and notices me, but didn't approach me. Months would go by and he continued to walk through the neighbourhood. Later I would find out that he would intentionally walk through my neighbourhood so he could catch glimpses of me sitting on the porch. Finally, he gets up the nerve to approach me. I didn't let him know, that I too, was noticing him. As we got to know one another I asked him a question. The question was "Why did you notice me?" He tells me "The reason I noticed you was because of how you always kept your son so neat and how you would just sit and hold your son." He told me he was so impressed with my dedication as a mom that it got his attention. Well, later I would marry this man and he took me away from the projects. Did I mention he adopted my son of three years old and gave my son his last name? I thank God for what he has done for me!! I thank God that He allowed me to go through what I went through, because now I'm wiser as a mom. My son is now thirty-six years of age. He is a college graduate. He has a business degree. He has three businesses. He was one of the youngest black men in Mississippi to become a Vice President of a bank. He also gives back to his community. I am so grateful for what the Lord has done and is doing in my life.

Even though my life is not the typical cookie cutter life, God used my life and the experiences of my life to propel me beyond my wildest dreams. We have two other children now, which are grown. But glory be to God, how He taught me early how to raise the other children. Had I not gone through the processing chambers in the projects, there would be no way that I could have gained the wisdom to guide my family through the rough times. My life may have started out shaky, but God was there the whole time. Today I am fifty-three years old. I've been married to my husband for thirty-two years. I am a college graduate. I have a major in Psychology and a minor in Communication. I pastor alongside my husband. I have a Talk Show called "She Speaks" that someday will be a household name. All because of the processing chamber in the projects. Don't despise the place you may be today, because God can still get the glory out of your life. Keep trusting God!

Romans 8:28
"And we know that all things work together for good to those who love GOD , to those who are the called according to His purpose."

Acknowledgements

First of all I want to thank the Lord who give me the desire to write this book regarding real mums' struggles and how Jesus helped and came into those mums' lives and changed them. I wholeheartedly want to thank all twenty-one mums from different nationalities who worked alongside me to make this book possible. They not only gave me permission to publish their testimonies, they also prayed with me as we all believe the Lord will use this book to demonstrate to you that motherhood is hard but Jesus is the one who give hope and Jesus has come into these mums' lives. I couldn't have done it without all those wonderful mums' help and they are now my friends so thank you so much and thank you Jesus for bringing them into my life.

About the Author

KoHsin Illingworth is the founder and director of Healed In Victory Ministry International. In the year of 2019 the Lord Jesus Christ told her to go out to the nations to testify for His name and since then her powerful testimony 'From HIV to Christ' has reached eighty-thousand viewers in Taiwan and continues to reach to Thailand, the United Kingdom and USA and, Glory to God, in 2020 it reached to the nations of Pakistan and India, Kenya , Africa and Malawi.

She is a passionate woman of God. She was a professional journalist in Taiwan, later on suffering from mental illness and almost dying from HIV/AIDS. Through a journey of Healing from Jesus Christ she become a professional interpreter in the UK. She is now an evangelist, speaker, a world traveller and mother of Hannah and believes God called her to run Healed in Victory ministry. She is now willing to preach the Gospel and thanks God she finally has a perfect family. Her great passion is to reach many people around the world with her testimony, to be a witness for Christ.

She is known to be determined, passionate and caring. She has spoken online and in person to many church meetings during the pandemic and she loves media evangelism. She is a pioneer for the Kingdom of God and an international speaker. She is now an engaging Christian speaker and hoping to influence and inspire people with the hope of Jesus Christ.

Printed in Great Britain
by Amazon

78008062R00079